RAPE
FIGHT BACK
AND
WIN
!

by
Captain James A. Smith

Stoeger Publishing Company
South Hackensack, New Jersey

Published by the Stoeger Publishing Company
55 Ruta Court, South Hackensack, New Jersey 07606

ISBN: 0-88317-119-8

Manufactured in the United States of America

Distributed to the book trade and to the sporting goods trade by Stoeger Industries, 55 Ruta Court, South Hackensack, New Jersey 07606.

In Canada, distributed to the book trade and to the sporting goods trade by Stoeger Canada Ltd., 165 Idema Road, Markham, Ontario L3R 1A9.

CONTENTS

ACKNOWLEDGMENTS

RAPE—FIGHT BACK AND WIN has taken over 25 years to put together. The acknowledgments would be far too numerous to include here, but I would like to thank the more than 400 women whom I have interviewed during the preparation of this book. Their comments and ideas were invaluable. I would also like to thank the countless law enforcement officers, the many Rape Crisis Centers and Victim Service Centers from all parts of this country and the world for their help.

RAPE—FIGHT BACK AND WIN is a continuation of my first book, "Rapist Beware" (published in 1978) and provides new and documented information for the women in this country and abroad to use in their fight against rape. I especially want to thank Chief of Police Sam Ivey of Lake Charles, Louisiana, for supporting me in my presentation of rape seminars throughout the U.S. I also want to thank the people of Colorado and Ohio where I served as police consultant for so many years. Their input was the basis for this book. I also want to thank the families of the victims involved in my research, and especially my own family members for their enthusiastic support and encouragement.

I would also like to give special recognition to the following models who appear in the book: Lenea Bruder; Paul Ellison; Debbie Cope; Beth Brooks; Juanita Wright; and Robert Smith. Thanks also go to the photographers, Myron Gilcher and Myron Klingensmith, to my editor, Dennis Weddle, and to the artist, Donna Dwigans.

FOREWORD

One of life's miracles is the fact that no two people are exactly alike. Even identical twins develop personality traits and physical characteristics that set them apart from one another. With all of our differences, however, we begin life with one very important common denominator: a brain to think and reason with. The difference lies in how we train our minds. Our parents may love and care for us as we progress through childhood, but they cannot think for us. This ability to think for ourselves is truly a wonderful thing, for it gives us the opportunity to develop those positive thought forces which can assure our very survival in this uncertain world. Your mind is like a garden — the seeds you plant in it will come forth inevitably, whether they be beautiful flowers or ugly weeds. It is very easy to think negative thoughts and let doubt and self-pity take over your life. If you think you cannot succeed, you probably won't.

What has all this to do with the subject of rape? Everything! The mind, you see, is the most important element in self-defense. In my talks and lectures to women throughout the country, I tell my listeners that they must prepare their minds properly if they wish to survive. No matter what age you are, I insist, it is possible to condition your mind and body to react positively to any challenge — including a rape attempt. And the first thing a woman must train her mind to do is *accept the fact that rape can happen to you, that it doesn't happen only to others.*

Accepting that fact doesn't mean you must live in fear or be a prisoner in your own home 24 hours a day.

Even if you were to install five locks on every door and train a Doberman pinscher to protect you, the possibility of rape exists. In this book, I will demonstrate how you can live a normal life without fear, because you have trained your mind to react in self-defense. But only you can make this happen. Reading my book will mean nothing if you do not follow through.

I'm reminded of an ancient Chinese proverb about a woman who asked her husband one day, "Why should I learn self-defense?" The husband replied, "If you came to a river and found a man starving and you had a basket of fish, would you give this man some fish?" The woman said, "Yes!"

But the husband responded, "No! Instead of feeding this man and satisfying him for only one meal, you should instead teach him how to fish. For then he can become self-reliant not only for the moment, but for the future."

The methods you will learn in this book for defending yourself in an emergency situation are intended to make you self-reliant. There is no judo or karate to learn here; there is only common sense and readiness to act. All I ask is that you spend a few minutes each day *conditioning your mind* so that it will respond instinctively when danger strikes. It could mean the difference between life and death, between mental health and emotional scars that last a lifetime, between a broken body and a sound one. The choice is yours — only you can make the decision to learn the lessons in this book or to ignore them at your peril.

Captain James A. Smith

CHAPTER 1

MEET THE RAPIST— HE IS EVERYWHERE!

Most women naturally think of rapists as demented human beings. The typical rapist is, in their eyes, a man who likes to sit alone in some darkened corner, perhaps masturbating or reading dirty books and magazines. He frequents X-rated moves and can be found lurking in dark hallways or hiding in the bushes at public parks. This image has been created and fostered by television, movies, books and articles, which in turn have caused potential victims to seek more information—or should I say *mis*information. This false image of the rapist is further enlarged by parents, friends, and acquaintances who may have come in contact with rape victims. By the time all of this information reaches the average woman, it is not only distorted and inaccurate—it can actually help build a wall between good men and women.

I have been associated with police work for over 25 years, and during that period I have investigated or interviewed over 350 women who were sexually assaulted or raped. In addition, I have talked to over 100 rapists, some of whom I helped send to jail (while others, unfortunately, were set free by a too lenient court system). From this experience I can state unequivocally that there is no set image that applies to all rapists. Many books and articles have been written by experts on the subject of rape, and many of these works have provided sound, well researched advice. While I do not claim to be a psychologist or a psychiatrist, I do have this first-hand field experience. It is something that cannot be measured statistically, but I know of no better "education" one could acquire concerning the psychological and physiological aspects of the rapist.

According to most well documented sources, 29 percent of all rapists are married men, and 19 to 22 percent of all rapes are committed by someone known to the victim—a friend or even a man whom the victim has dated. I have also read that 5.6 percent of all rapes are committed against hitchhikers. That may seem like a terribly inaccurate statistic to someone who lives in a community where 51 percent of all rape vic-

tims are known to be hitchhikers. If that sounds confusing, take a moment to think about the countless demographic areas that exist within the United States. In a congested urban area with a high rate of crime, rape will obviously be much more prevalent than in a rural community with a sparse population. Different parts of the country can have a tremendous effect on statistical accuracy. For example, in a small town of 5,000 people or less, where everyone knows his or her neighbors, a stranger is quickly noticed. The police, sheriff, or constable in that town will also spot the outsider in a hurry. The chances of a rapist succeeding there are obviously less than in a crowded city. Conversely, many popular recreational areas which are normally quiet and crime-free during the off-season can become highly dangerous places once the tourists arrive. The problem of rape suddenly becomes more acute along with most other criminal activities. Military bases are also subject to the problem of sexual assault or rape. During the summer season, an oceanside town whose winter population is less than 5,000 can balloon to 50,000 or more in a matter of days. These visitors come to drink and enjoy themselves, often releasing their inhibitions with the aid of alcohol and other drugs. Under these conditions, it should not be surprising to find an increase in the number of sexual assaults and rapes.

My point is, the rape statistics we read about may be helpful to some, but all too often assaults and rapes are not reported. As a result, no one really knows how many rapes actually occur. The figure could be as high as 100 unreported rapes for each one that is reported. I know of one example where a prisoner who had committed rape was arrested on over eight occasions. He was able to beat the charges each time except on his last arrest. Later, he bragged to a fellow inmate that during a six-year period he had raped over 300 women and personally felt lucky to have been sentenced to only 10 to 20 years. Most of his victims, he confessed, had never reported the crimes. He picked out only certain women and each act was carefully planned (as are most rapes). His victims were mostly in the 19 to 25 age group — typically women who frequented bars or clubs after work. Physically, this man was considered "normal and nice looking," so he was able to set up his victims with great care and least risk.

One of the most blatant rape cases took place in Ocala, Florida, in March of 1983. A traffic accident involving 22 cars had caused four deaths and 27 injuries. The road was covered with smoke and fire from cars exploding, and soon hundreds of police and fire rescue personnel were at the scene. During the confusion and the long wait in traffic, a 23-year-old woman driver was raped, then shoved out of her car when traffic began to move. She had been stabbed several times. The police thought at first she had been a victim of the accident, until she was able to tell them what happened.

So you can see why it is almost impossible to say this percentage or that applies when it comes to the subject of rape. We do know for certain that rape does happen, and that women are raped for many reasons. What we will deal with in this book is the assault itself, and a woman's defense against it. Most behavioral scientists agree that the typical rapist is not interested in the thrill and satisfaction of the sex act itself; his twisted mind is primarily concerned with power and the total domination of his victim. Hundreds of different reasons are given by psychiatrists, psychologists, and case workers as to what causes a man to rape. This book will not deal with these matters. It will deal with the victim's response to the rape attempt and how to prevent its onset.

All too often when a rape occurs the guilty man knows he will not be caught and convicted. The reasons why are limited only by the imagination. Suppose the victim herself has been involved in an illegal activity, such as dealing in drugs. She cannot go to the police without disclosing her own culpability. Nor is it likely that a rape victim who is going through an illegal abortion, or who is performing illegal abortions, will report her rape. I have heard of men raping their brothers' wives; the victims, knowing how their husbands will react, usually decide not to say anything for fear of repercussions within the family. Estranged husbands occasionally come back to rape their own wives, and again the victim fails to report the crime. After all, who will take her seriously? As long as no serious violence is involved in these cases, the wife will usually "go along" with the situation and suffer in silence. I have heard many stories like these told by wives, sisters, and other female relatives. When asked why they did not report the crimes, they answer, "I was afraid for my husband," or, "I was afraid it would destroy my marriage and family." It is her word against her attacker's. I know of other women who have reported the rape but refused to sign a complaint. In some instances, a burglar has entered an apartment while the victim is sleeping. When she awakens, the thief tries to keep her quiet. When she cries out in fear and panic, he assaults her out of anger.

The Four Stages of Rape

All rape acts pass through at least one of four different stages or levels, the first and most common of which is called *possession.* In this stage the male wishes to possess the female against her will. He starts out by trying to learn all about his victim's habits — when she picks up her newspaper, empties the trash, goes to the corner store, or turns off the lights at night. That is why it is so important for vulnerable women to change their habits periodically. Don't use the same parking space every day; don't wear name tags with your real name; don't take the same route home from work or school every night.

It is during the possession stage that the woman has the greatest advantage. She can turn around the man's desire to assault, degrade, and humiliate her and use it against him. In the following pages, you will see how a potential victim of sexual assault manages to escape by playing on the man's gullibility and desire.

Defense by Playing on Male Gullibility

(When a Friend or Date Won't Take "NO" for an Answer)

In this instance the man places his hand on the victim's leg, attempting to arouse her despite her repeated efforts to repel his attentions. Using his own gullibility, the victim can extricate herself from the situation.

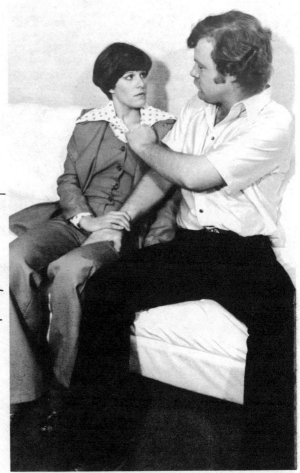

The attacker puts one hand between the victim's legs and the other on her blouse. Lacking the physical strength to break loose, the victim must play on his sexual intentions to defeat him. Putting her hand on top of the hand on her leg, the victim bends it and weakens his grip; at the same time she gazes into his eyes to distract him.

Still gazing into the attacker's eyes, the victim lifts the hand from her leg and asks the attacker to kiss her—at the same time, turning him toward her breast. While doing this, she puts her free hand over his, locks his arm against her upper arm, and prepares for a defensive move.

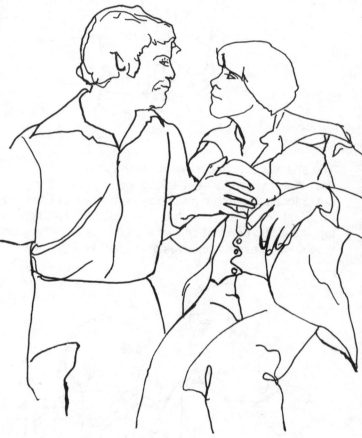

Above: The attacker's hand is on the victim's breast—but locked firmly between the victim's two hands with his elbow immobilized against her upper arm. Below: She continues to hold his gaze, and as he moves forward to kiss her, the victim exerts pressure on the attacker's knuckles, freezing him with such pain that he will be unable to strike her with his free hand. Now she can order him out, or march him to the door, her hold on him still clamped into place.

This photograph illustrates the position to assume when attacked while seated and afraid of being injured. The victim expresses her terror and promises her cooperation, firing his imagination by suggesting oral sex. She then drops her head limply against his chest, while forming the spear hand (hand flat with the ends of the fingers bent).

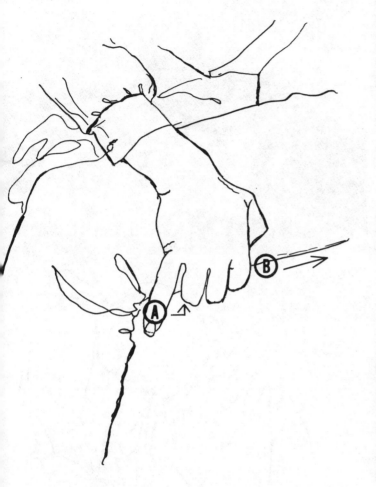

With her head in this position, the attacker cannot see what the victim is doing. She places her hand on the inside of his leg—perhaps exciting him—the little finger between the kneecap and the surface of the seat (A). Rotating the knuckles toward the groin, she aims toward the testicles, following the surface of the seat rather than the contour of his leg (B) to be sure of striking the target and causing the most damage.

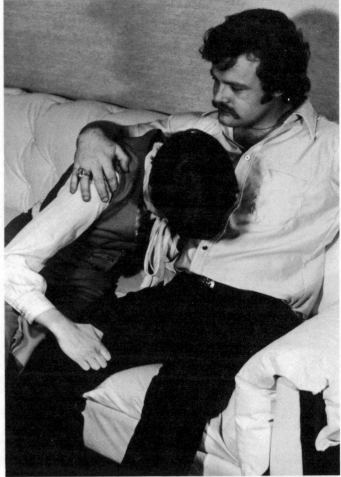

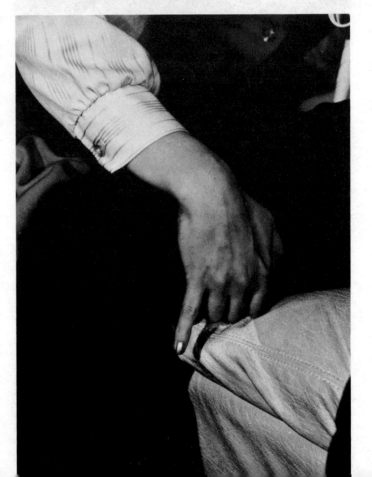

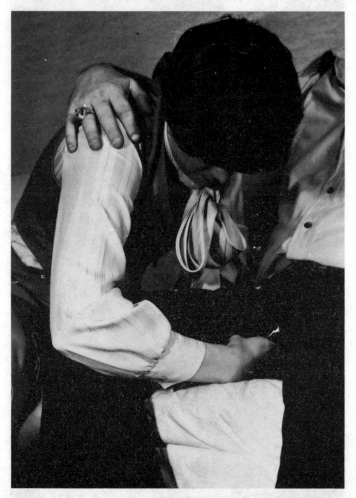

Upper right: The spear hand is formed with fingers bent and thumb down. In the other illustrations, the spear hand drives at the attacker's testicles, hugging the contour of the seat for greatest accuracy in striking. The victim may have to stall the attacker by cooperating to the point where he has removed his trousers—in which case such a blow is even more debilitating and effective. In this position, she can also smash the top of her head into his face.

worse by striking an assailant in this area. Why should you want to take the life of a rapist? That is, of course, a matter for each reader to decide. It's possible to be attacked by a "normal" rapist and come through the ordeal without serious injury. Then again, you could be the victim of a frustrated rapist, a man who has not enjoyed fulfillment recently and who therefore is in the mood to inflict pain on you. I have viewed the mutilated bodies of girls who did not make it, and as a result I have always sworn that, if I were a victim, I would use everything at my disposal to protect myself.

The ABC's of Self-Defense

What is the first thing you would do if you came home one night and found a strange man in your house? Or what if you were already home and he forced his way in? My advice is: *grab any object and throw it through the nearest window, then immediately begin to scream at the top of your voice.* Breaking glass may seem silly, but it has proven very effective. The sound of breaking glass frightens intruders and your screams are a reminder that help may soon be on the way. When you do scream, however, never scream RAPE! Most people within earshot will not want to become involved, mostly because they fear for their own lives. Their attitude is, "Let someone else do it!" What you *should* scream is FIRE! Now you have dramatically and personally affected everyone around you, for suddenly their homes, families, and possessions are at stake.

Weapons — such as guns, knives, tear gas cannisters and the like — are generally not effective deterrents to rape. In most cases, such weapons are not handy when needed; and even if they are, there is always a good chance they will be taken from you and used against you. Tear gas may stop a rapist temporarily, but the fumes could injure you as well as the intruder. Besides, all he has to do is throw a coat or jacket over the cannister — then where are you?

My advice is, first *use the gullibility of the male* to best advantage. Remember too that *rape takes time*

(see also p. 8). The longer you resist, the better your chance of escaping or scaring off your attacker. Should the rapist confront you with a gun or knife, I suggest that you submit to him until you are in a position to do something about it — even if that means having involuntary intercourse. We will tell you more about what to do under these circumstances in Chapters 12 and 13. I should mention also that many rapists, aware of how much a woman values her face, will use that vulnerability to their advantage. I have found that a woman who would not ordinarily submit to a rapist when other parts of her body were threatened will do so when her face is endangered. Sharp instruments, such as broken glass or beer can openers, are not considered "dangerous weapons" under the law. On the other hand, sexual assault by force is a major crime calling for 40 years to life in prison. More terrible still to a woman is the fear that the rapist will attack a third party, particularly a child or other close relatives. Under these grim circumstances, my only advice is to submit to the rapist's demands unless or until help arrives.

I have held classes on self-defense against rape all over the country and have talked to women from all walks of life. Many of them work in environments that are more susceptible to assault attempts — waitresses, nurses, apartment house managers, telephone operators, and yes, even prostitutes. I always impress upon these women the importance of practicing the techniques taught in this book with their friends, boyfriends, or husbands. In doing so, however, I must urge caution, for you could injure your partner severely. These defensive techniques should be kept in the back of your mind and used as a weapon only when an actual assault is attempted. I've also included some tips on how to handle "peeping toms" and obscene phone callers. While they may seem harmless enough, these men frequently progress to more aggressive tactics, including rape. Always keep your window shades or curtains drawn at night, and don't run around in your home scantily clad. Use common sense and avoid activities that tend to make you more susceptible.

In the following pages, you will learn all of my methods, step by step, for defeating the rapist — from the initial grab to the attack itself. Most of you will be forced to use your imagination and practice these techniques on your own. As for judo and karate, I have been teaching these sports for 27 years, but I must tell you that they are practically useless, especially in the back seat of a car or some other confined area. It will not help much to say to your attacker, "Stand up, please, so I can throw you!" We do, however, use some forms of these techniques involving the hand, knee, elbow, foot, and head.

Soon you will feel much more confident about protecting yourself and preventing an assault. I hope also that I've dispelled forever the myth that a woman should never provoke the anger of a rapist. It is far better to protect yourself as I've described, and have a few bruises and cuts to show for it, than to become still another crime statistic. Remember, your attacker wants to dominate you and have power over you. By telling him initially that you are afraid and do not want to get hurt, you are buying time and satisfying the man's overriding desire for possession. During this period, you may have to say things that you normally would not say. But sometimes you may even talk him out of the rape, although that doesn't happen very often. In most cases, you will have to rely on your wits, your strength, and your attacker's physical vulnerabilities.

The Time Factor

The question is often asked, "How long does it take on average for an act of rape?" To the woman who must go through the ordeal, the answer is most likely "an eternity." Still, to those women who have no direct experience, the question reflects a natural concern and should be addressed.

According to most experts and available data, the average time to complete a rape is from 1½ hours to four hours. That may seem almost unbelievably long, but to those who have survived the experience it will come as no surprise. The California Rape Crisis Center reports that the average duration of a rape attack in that state is about four hours. The Chicago area has indicated much the same thing. I have, in turn, interviewed more than 400 rape victims from coast to coast, plus several from outside the U.S. Accordingly, I have come to the following conclusions regarding the time factor: (1) the rapist must forcibly maneuver his victim into the proper position for penetration; (2) some or all of the clothes must be removed, from his own body as well as his victim's; (3) the rapist must be aroused physically to complete the sex act; (4) the victim must also be aroused, if only out of fear, so as to produce involuntary secretions; and (5) certain psychological, physiological, and biological events must take place before penetration is possible. All of this takes time — and often it takes a lot of time.

In my years of interviewing rape victims, there has been only one case in which the rape lasted less than 20 minutes. I have also interviewed many rapists as well, and in my experience the myth that the victim's struggling excites the rapist sexually is just that — a myth. If fighting back did indeed excite the rapist, we might well have a readily available cure for the 4,000,000 men in our society who are, according to most estimates, being treated for impotence. These men could be cured merely by instructing their sex partners to fight, scratch, or kick them until they were aroused. On the contrary, these actions by their victims actually prevent or at least slow down the rapist's ability to complete the act. Techniques such as biting, kicking, hitting, or using a key to gouge an attacker's face and eyes are not likely to get a normal man sexually excited, much less a rapist.

To comprehend this matter of time even better, look at your watch for a few minutes. Did you ever imagine

18

two minutes could take that long? Knowing that the average rape takes from 20 minutes to several hours, don't you feel confident that with the proper knowledge and training you could do something to protect yourself from a rapist—especially with your very life in danger?

One bitter fact bears repeating: more women die from sexual assault each year than from both fire and drownings combined. Equally important to remember is that rapists do *not* wear signs. You have no idea what type of a man you will have to deal with should the time ever come. There are perverted rapists, sadistic rapists, and killer rapists. If you need convincing, just study your local newspaper for about a month and keep track of how many people die from fires and drownings as opposed to those who have been tried and convicted of homicide as a result of sexual assaults. You will be amazed. And yet, sad as this statistic may be, only about five to ten percent of all rapes are actually reported, while almost all deaths due to fire and drownings are. Here's another one: each year about one million girls and boys run away from home, and of these some 25,000 under the age 16 are never heard from again. Officials estimate that about 5,000 of these are young girls who are killed as a result of sexual assault.

Do these figures scare you? Good! Rape is not the delicate subject it once was, fortunately, so we can now talk about it openly and, more important, devise ways for women to defend themselves. In the pages to follow we will teach you how to react to any given situation, how to prevent an assault before it happens, and what to do during an assault. For example, many rapes take place with the victim face down on her stomach.

That way, it will be more difficult for her to identify the assailant later as to his facial features, hair color, scars, or clothing. We will show you several effective ways to fight off a rapist from that prone position.

The National Institute on Rape, which is headquartered in Washington, D.C., advises that women who fight back, who resist and are aggressive no matter what their size and strength, usually *do* prevent the rape from occurring. Occasionally some injuries may be sustained, such as getting punched or cut by the attacker, but at least these women have protected themselves from the ultimate degradation; they did not plead with or give in to their attackers' desires. On the other hand, those victims who remain passive and do not resist stand a good chance of ending up in the morgue.

Consider this: if you were in a fire, would you lie there and hope that the firemen would arrive in time to save you? Or would you take some kind of positive action to protect yourself from injury and possible death, even though you knew it was dangerous? If you were drowning, would you simply allow yourself to sink to the bottom and die? Or would you try to save yourself using any means at hand? The answers are obvious. By the same token, rape is a life-threatening situation, the same as fire and drowning; you should therefore know and use every method possible to save yourself.

There is one circumstance, however, where I must caution you *never* to try defending yourself against a rapist: *when he is armed.* If a rapist has a weapon at your throat, he will probably use it if necessary. In that situation, your only recourse is to submit to the rape until help arrives or the rapist grows careless and allows you to escape.

CHAPTER 2

WHAT SHOULD I TELL MY CHILD ABOUT RAPE?

This book was written not only for the adult female but for young women from 9 to 19. As a proud parent myself, I wish it were not necessary to discuss the grim subject of rape with youngsters, and often I have wished fervently that the crime itself would somehow disappear. Unfortunately, this will probably never happen, at least not in our lifetimes. As parents, I fear we too often adopt a "head in the sand" attitude about such unpleasant topics as rape and child molesting, perhaps in the hope that by not talking about the seamier aspects of life they may simply go away. That wish does not, of course, jibe with reality. As mentioned in the previous chapter, almost 5,000 teenage and pre-teenage runaway girls are killed by sexual assault each year. This figure does not include all those who die by sexual assault who are *not* runaways.

You and I, as parents and/or guardians, have certain responsibilities in bringing up our children. This includes not only their physical needs — such as providing food, shelter, and clothing — but the monumental task of dealing with the emotional and psychological aspects of their lives. For too long now, in my opinion, we have left the subject of sex education solely in the hands of our school systems — especially such sensitive areas as rape, incest, and child molestation. Unfortunately, our educational institutions have done a poor job in most cases of explaining these delicate matters to our youth. Our most common excuse for this failure is that children under 16 or so are too young to deal with such shocking truths. In fact, it is we, the parents, who cannot handle these subjects. We then try to justify our failure by saying something like this: "I don't want to put such terrible

ideas in my child's head," or, "I'll wait until he or she is a little older." Do these remarks sound familiar to you? They should.

The truth is, we parents are guilty of not giving our children straight answers to straight questions about sexual assault. As soon as our children are able to comprehend, we have no trouble telling them, "Don't play with matches! You may start a fire!" And when the child asks why, we immediately answer, "Because fire is dangerous, and you could be burned to death or injure other people." Another familiar parent-child dialogue goes like this: "Don't go too near the water"... "Why, Mommy and Daddy?"..."Because you could drown and die."

Children will accept these answers because they look up to us as parents, and because they believe we know what is best for them. The trouble is, when a dialogue arises concerning rape and child molesting, most parents abandon the direct, common-sense approach. Instead, they admonish the child: "Don't ever talk to strangers!" And when the child responds, "Why, Mommy and Daddy?", we reply, "Because I told you not to. Some people are not nice."

I believe the reason most of us are guilty of this poor response stems from our own inability to accept the fact that rape, incest, and other violations happen all the time. As parents, we have a tremendous responsibility to make sure that our children understand the full extent of danger that awaits an unsuspecting child. Your daughter has a right to know the facts about sexual assault and what she can do to avoid it. Do not make the mistake of assuming she is too young to understand. I recommend to parents of girls ten and under that they simply explain to their daughters that some men are sick and may try to hurt them physically. Most children in that age bracket can relate to this physical aspect because they have been spanked by their parents or have been involved in fights with their peers. They know what it's like to be hurt and they want to avoid it if at all possible. So when a stranger approaches them and tries to coax them into a car or touch them, they should be taught to run away, scream, attract attention. They should not walk home from school alone or go out at night without an adult.

For girls 11 and over, I advocate talking openly about the sexual aspects of rape. A young girl should never allow a man to touch her private parts; she must kick, scream, and fight as hard as she can to escape when accosted. Children today are much more knowledgeable about sex at an earlier age than we can imagine. The world has changed and we must change with it. The old "head in the sand" syndrome won't work any longer.

If you doubt that our modern teenagers and sub-teens are not exposed to more information about sexual matters than you and I were at the same age, take a look at what goes on in the popular television shows and movies they watch, and the books and magazines they read. Some cable television programs feature R and even X-rated films now. We are being very naive indeed if we believe that our 11 and 12-year-old daughters have not been exposed to some sort of sexually explicit material. Any inquisitive child can find a way to "sneak a peek" at a late night cable TV movie — especially in a home where both mother and father are working.

So let's face it, Mom and Dad, the days of childhood innocence have passed and we must accept the responsibility of giving our children accurate, straightforward information about how to deal with sexual assault situations.

Another ill-conceived approach is one most fathers are guilty of. It goes something like this: "If I ever catch anyone touching my daughter, I'll kill him!" There is no way you can hold your daughter prisoner for 24 hours a day to insure her safety. Would you let your daughter swim at a community pool or public beach without a qualified lifeguard on duty? Of course not. And yet, your daughter has a far greater chance of being raped or sexually molested than she does of drowning.

The bottom line on this subject is this: give your daughter the knowledge she needs if and when she is ever confronted by a rapist. Let her know what she can do to prevent such an occurrence *before* it becomes a nightmare that can scar her emotionally for life. Consider the information in this book just as vital as the fire drill she gets at school. It will *not* warp her thinking or make her more interested in sex than she already is. What it will do is help prevent her from becoming a statistic in some future police crime report. The information we offer can give her a chance to understand what can happen out there, and how to cope with bad situations as they arise. Fear of the unknown is often worse than reality. You owe it to your daughter to give her the right information so that she can cope with this negative aspect of life in a positive, life-saving way.

CHAPTER **3**

THE TRUTH ABOUT MACE, TEAR GAS, AND OTHER CHEMICAL DEFENSES AGAINST RAPE

Hundreds, perhaps thousands, of chemical sprays which claim to deter rapists and muggers are being sold throughout the U.S. Some even promise that "you will be able to stop one to ten or more men at a distance of fifteen feet." Such claims are useful only to the manufacturers who seek to increase sales and profits, and they should be treated as such by the public at large. The people who sell these products naturally want us to feel more confident and safe; but their claims of rendering attackers harmless or of crippling their nervous systems are generally not true. Most recent tests indicate that chemical sprays are simply not effective deterrents against attack.

The sad fact is, the street-wise rapist or mugger has long since developed techniques with which to overcome these potential hazards. The attacker has only to throw a jacket or similar object over the spray can in order to render it harmless. Temperature and wind factors also come into play, as well as other natural conditions that can diminish the effectiveness of such chemicals. One popular spray is carried on a key ring, where it can be easily spotted by an attacker. Moreover, spray cans frequently rupture or explode, causing accidents and injury. Children have been known to pick up and play with these devices, thereby endangering their health and safety.

Consider also the potential risks involved in the manufacturers' claims that attackers can be stopped at a distance of 10 feet with these sprays. In most cases, a woman who stands 10 feet from a strange man does not yet feel threatened. Only when her potential enemy comes within close range or makes a sudden move toward her does she know for certain that a dangerous situation exists. By then, it is probably too late to haul out a spray can and use it effectively. Besides, if everyone listened to these sales pitches, there could well be an epidemic of semi-hysterical people running around spraying each other indiscriminately.

Many police and law enforcement agencies have, in fact, stopped carrying the chemical sprays. The International Association of Chiefs of Police made a study a few years ago and found that out of 339 cases police who were armed with clubs or similar weapons won out every time over those using mace or tear gas.

For those who insist on using chemical sprays, but don't want to spend more than ten dollars for them, I recommend the following substitutes: a pressurized can of oven cleaner (with lye as an ingredient) or hair spray; a pressurized aerosol can of Lysol; or a pesticide such as Raid. These products work very well and can be kept conveniently in the home, car, or even a large handbag. Spray one of these products into the face of an intruder and he will be forced to cover his eyes. He may even be blinded temporarily, giving you ample time to escape. But, as we have noted elsewhere in this book, the best solution of all is to buy a small, two-pound Halon gas fire extinguisher and keep it near your front or back door. Carry one in your car, too. These extinguishers have a range of about 15 feet and are very effective. They can also produce a spray (about 100 pounds per square inch) that is far more powerful than any commercial spray product on the market. By the way, do your front and back doors have peepholes installed in them? If not, they should — it's always a good idea to see who is outside before opening the door to anyone.

The small fire extinguisher I've recommended is not expensive, can be bought in several different sizes, and can be used for more than self-defense. It is also a great safety product to have in any home. As for the cannister sprays discussed in this chapter, they will do just as well as, if not better than, such chemicals as mace and tear gas. But be sure to carry *something* with you at all times. Remember, a man has to bend over in order to enter any car built today. Thus, you are in a perfect position to aim your spray can at the attacker's face and hit him full blast with it. You can then follow up by thrusting your car key in his face or throat. That should stop the attacker and give you time to drive away or seek safety elsewhere.

No single defense is best, of course; you must use whatever opportunities present themselves at the time. If a rapist has managed to enter your home before you can sound an alarm, break some glass and scream FIRE! Then make your move for the spray can or extinguisher. Every situation is different and circumstances vary tremendously. Think to yourself as you read these pages which methods you would use given the need. Plant the seeds in your mind and they will emerge instinctively as the emergency arises. We all tend to freeze momentarily in times of stress; but the more you think ahead about how you will react in certain situations, the less chance you'll have of not being able or ready to respond at all. The trained mind is prepared to act in any emergency situation. It thus becomes a means of self-defense; indeed, the very reaon we place such thoughts into our minds is to assure our very *survival*. After all, isn't that the name of this deadly game?

CHAPTER 4

DEFENSE AGAINST MOST COMMON ATTACKS FROM THE REAR

In the pages and chapters to follow, we will show in pictorial fashion exactly how the potential rape victim can extricate herself from dangerous and even life-threatening situations. These range from attacks on elevators and darkened hallways to bedrooms and automobiles; they cover attacks from the rear and the side; and they show how to ward off rapists with only the keys to one's house or car as a weapon.

By studying these photographs and drawings carefully, and by practicing the various techniques as illustrated, we feel confident that you will be able to defend yourself successfully in time of need. In some instances, the pictures are not very pleasant to look at — but then, rape is not a pleasant subject. When a man attacks you without warning and threatens to violate your very soul and body, you will not hesitate to inflict the violent and painful defensive blows shown here, I can assure you. There simply is no "nice" way to go about this.

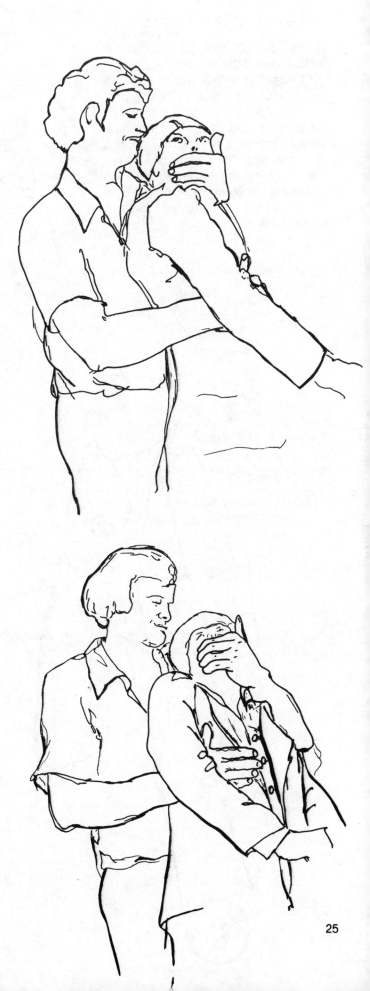

Most rapists will initiate their attack by placing one hand over the victim's mouth, to prevent the victim from screaming, and the other hand over her breast. Since the victim's first reaction is to remove the rapist's hand from her breast, the rapist will use the hand which is over the victim's mouth to try to choke her. Once the victim ceases to resist, the attacker will proceed with his rape.

In this assault, the victim's head is turned toward the attacker's upper left arm. Grasping the attacker's right hand, which is on her breast (right), the victim brings her right leg forward (see below). Raising her free arm straight in front, palm up, while turning her head, she pivots on the balls of her feet, enabling her to deliver a strong backward blow with her right elbow (D). With the arm turned down, a strong blow is impossible.

A side view showing the victim's clenched fist (A) before her elbow drives back into the target area—the would-be rapist's exposed stomach (B). Note how the victim's head is turned toward the attacker's upper arm (C) and how her body is twisted with the arm kept close to her side for extra strength in delivering the blow (below).

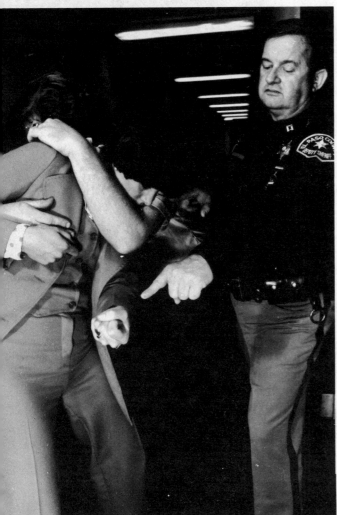

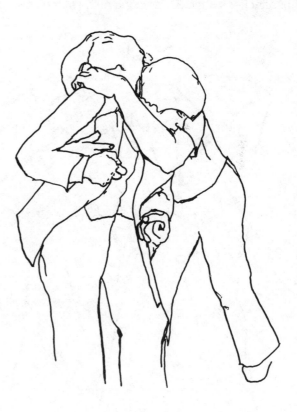

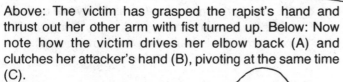

Above: The victim has grasped the rapist's hand and thrust out her other arm with fist turned up. Below: Now note how the victim drives her elbow back (A) and clutches her attacker's hand (B), pivoting at the same time (C).

While retaining a grip on the attacker's hand (A), her chin in the crook of his arm (B), and her feet still pivoted (C), the victim swerves her hips away and slashes the blade of her hand into the attacker's groin (D).

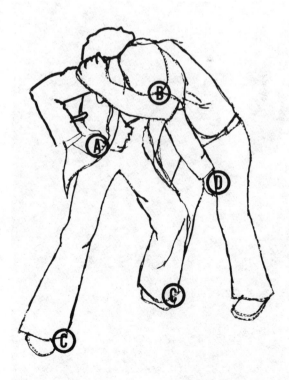

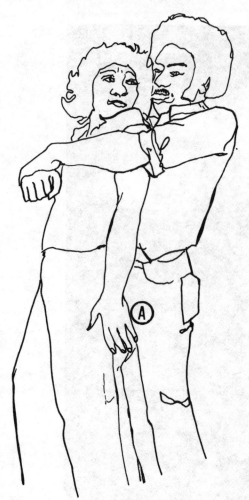

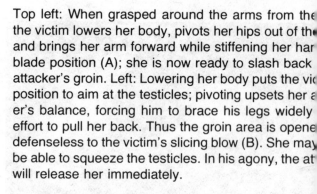
Top left: When grasped around the arms from the the victim lowers her body, pivots her hips out of the and brings her arm forward while stiffening her har blade position (A); she is now ready to slash back attacker's groin. Left: Lowering her body puts the vic position to aim at the testicles; pivoting upsets her a er's balance, forcing him to brace his legs widely effort to pull her back. Thus the groin area is opene defenseless to the victim's slicing blow (B). She may be able to squeeze the testicles. In his agony, the at will release her immediately.

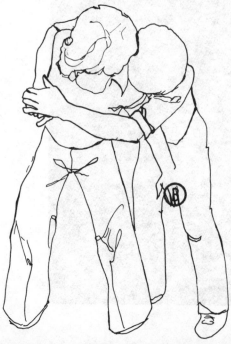

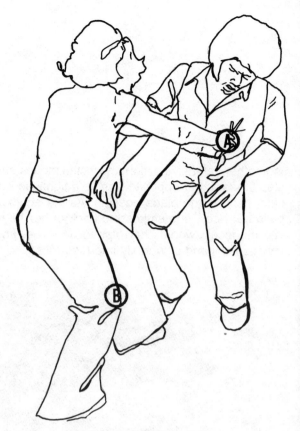

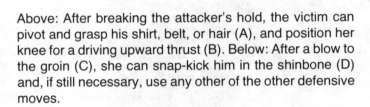

Above: After breaking the attacker's hold, the victim can pivot and grasp his shirt, belt, or hair (A), and position her knee for a driving upward thrust (B). Below: After a blow to the groin (C), she can snap-kick him in the shinbone (D) and, if still necessary, use any other of the other defensive moves.

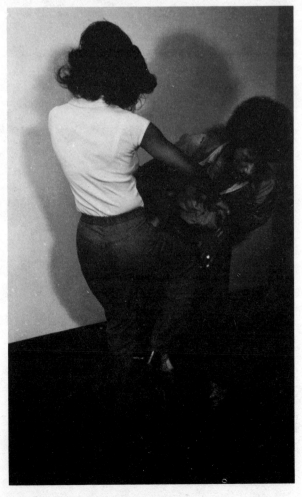

In another defensive action, the victim moves one step forward, her opposite arm held tightly to her side, hand in the blade position. As the attacker pulls her back, she strikes the back of her head into his face, swerves her hips to one side, and swings her hand powerfully into his groin.

Defense Against Rear Grasp of the Body or Breast

The attacker grabs the victim from the rear, his hands on her breasts, his body pressed against hers. Terrifying as such an attack may be, the victim's fear and anger can stimulate her to resist.

The victim should not try to tear the attacker's hands from her breasts, as instinct might dictate. Instead, the victim straightens her body, bringing her hand down with palm facing back (A), and drops her head forward.

The victim quickly flings her head back, striking the nose and face of her attacker (A), keeping her body straight. The blow should cause him to drop his hands from her breasts—at least as far as her waistline. Next, the victim reaches back and squeezes her attacker's testicles (B), using her other hand to grasp his shirt to keep him upright in case she needs to strike him again.

CHAPTER 5

Defense Against Underarm Grasp

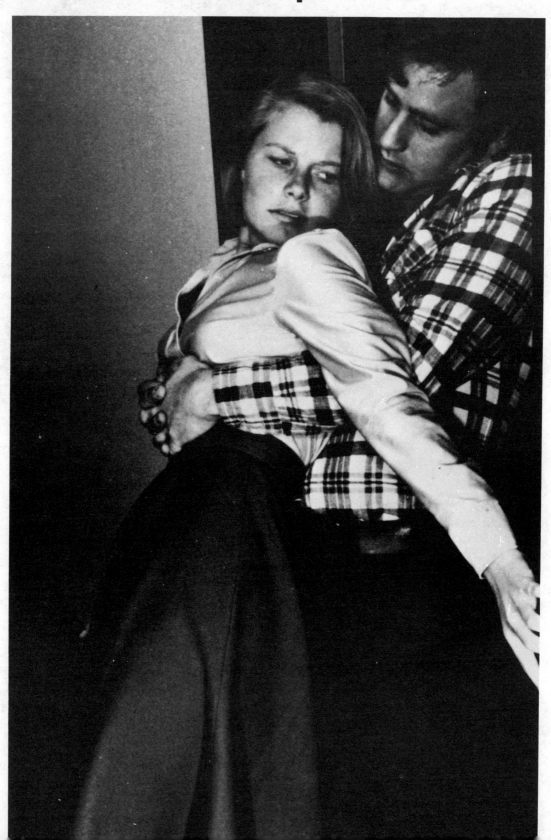

In this defensive move, the victim maintains her balance, turns her head toward the attacker, and screams as loud as she can at him. While screaming, the victim makes a fist, blocking the knuckles with her thumb for greater strength when striking a blow (lower left).

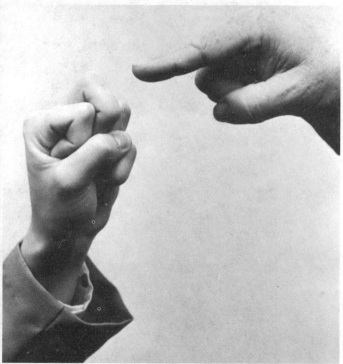

Bringing her hands 10 to 12 inches away from her body
(A), the victim takes a step forward (B). This movement
makes the attacker pull the victim back, which stretches
and exposes his hands (E and F).

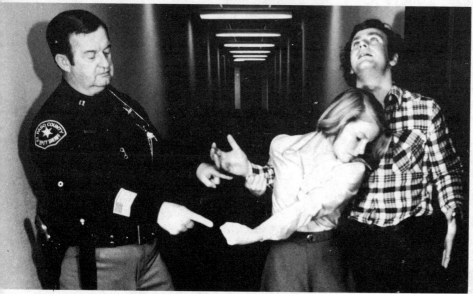

Top: The victim strikes the exposed backs of the attacker's hands with her knuckles. This causes extreme pain and may actually break some of the smaller bones. (The fist-and-knuckle technique can be used on any part of the body.)

Bottom: After striking the attacker's hands, the victim brings her left arm forward, fist up (C); grabs the attacker's right sleeve or wrist (B), holding it tightly to her side; and steps forward with her right foot.

Top: The victim now pivots, moving her hips away from the attacker, and jabs her left elbow (B) into the attacker's stomach.

Bottom: An alternative move: While still firmly holding onto the attacker's sleeve, the victim pivots, pushes the attacker against the wall, and drives her knee into his groin.

Above: In another defense against the underarm grasp, the victim immediately falls forward, dropping her head and her upper body. Below: Then, gathering her strength, she smashes the back of her head into the attacker's face, which could fracture his jaw or nose, or at least cause him excruciating pain. Turning, the victim now uses any of the previous techniques.

Defense Against Two-Handed Grab

When both hands are captured and the attacker drags the victim toward him, she should pull back, keeping one leg behind her, and make him pull her even harder. Then, swinging her rear leg forward, she drives her knee up into the attacker's groin. Once the attacker has fallen, the victim can stomp his neck, grasping his shirt to retain her balance (below).

When the victim resists the attacker's drag, he has to pull her toward himself. At this instant, she steps forward and drives her knee into his groin (as illustrated below). Grabbing his hair helps to gain control. Or, the victim can smash the top of her head into his nose while grasping his shirt to bring him closer. The victim can also hit her head against his mouth, depending on her speed and agility.

Here the victim drives her forehead at her attacker's face first, following up with a knee to the groin—a technique which should stop any attack.

A rapist frequently attacks from the rear, gripping the victim low under the arms, with his leg braced against her, and his body pressed sensuously to hers. In this position, it is sometimes difficult to reach back and strike the attacker. The victim can pound his hands with her knuckled fists to break his hold. Or, the victim can push her hips forward and then powerfully thrust the buttocks into his pelvis. The shock of pain ought to make the attacker release the victim.

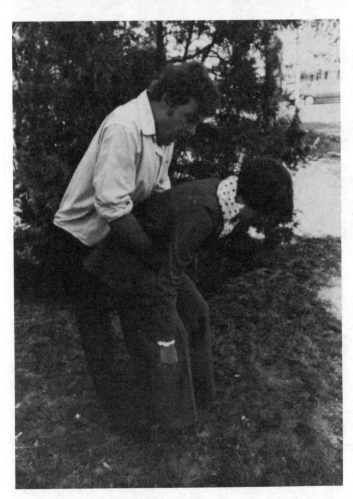

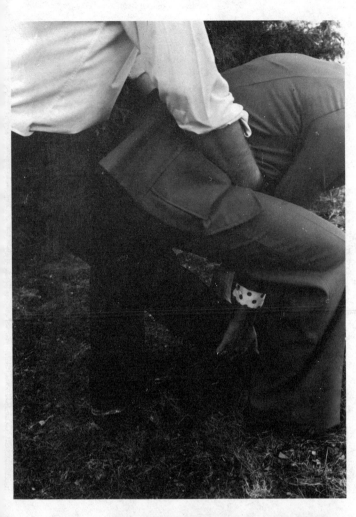

If, after thrusting her buttocks back, the victim is still gripped around her waist, she should follow with a sudden drop directly on top of the attacker's knee. Grasping his pants leg or ankle, pull his leg up, thus toppling him.

The attacker will land on either his spine or his head. While still holding onto his foot, the victim pivots and drives the heel of her shoe into his testicles, groin area, or throat.

If the attacker grabs his victim by her lapel and brings his other fist back to strike her, the victim should grab the arm or sleeve of the arm holding her and side-kick the attacker's kneecap or stomach. Screaming "KIAI" into the attacker's face should throw him sufficiently off balance to enable the victim to follow through with a knee to his groin. Another method of breaking the attacker's hold on the victim's lapel is to strike the hand holding the victim with the knuckles.

The victim has pulled the attacker toward her by the sleeve and kicked with all her strength at his kneecap—possibly fracturing, at least injuring, it and the shinbone. Still clutching the attacker, the victim forms a blade hand, this time with the thumb turned outward.

At this point the victim steps forward and drives her thumb and the blade of her hand into her attacker's trachea. Since this blow can be fatal, caution is advised when practicing.

Defense Against Arm Drags

When gripped by one hand and dragged by an attacker, the victim should pull back and then immediately step forward, throwing her attacker off balance. She can then smash the knuckles of her free hand against the back of his hand; snap-kick him in the groin, the kneecap, or the shin; or drive her forehead into his face. The important point to remember is to pull back when dragged and then step forward at once, slackening the tension and unbalancing the attacker.

If the victim is grasped by both hands and dragged forward by an attacker, she should again resist and then suddenly move in at him—now in perfect position to snap-kick him in the groin or the kneecap with her toe or the heel of her foot. Or, having stepped forward, she can drop suddenly to the ground and, as he bends over to pull her up, drive her knee upward into his groin, following through with a snap kick to the kneecap or a butt with her head into his face.

A snap kick to the instep can also inflict a painful injury, as can stomping on the instep, which may even break the attacker's foot. A kick to the kneecap can fracture or dislocate it.

When the victim's wrist is caught in a two-handed grip, she should bend her knees, forcing the attacker to pull her toward himself even harder. Then she strikes her knuckles against the back of his hand, inflicting enough pain to break his hold.

Having struck the attacker's hand with her knuckles, the victim then kicks the side of her foot at his knee, scraping all the way down the leg.

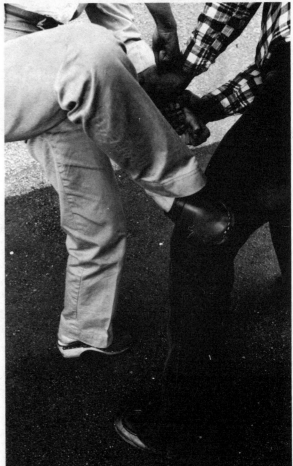

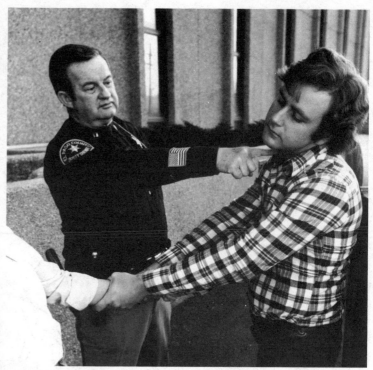

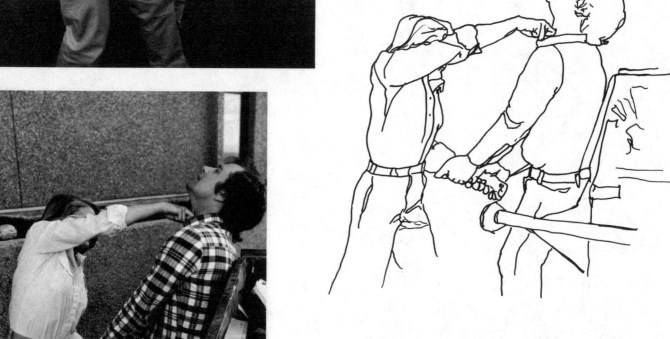

When the attacker uses a two-handed grip, both hands are occupied. As he drags the victim toward him, she takes the knuckled V position with her free hand, keeping her palm up. Then, as she strikes at his windpipe, she twists her hand for additional power, making her blow as crippling as possible.

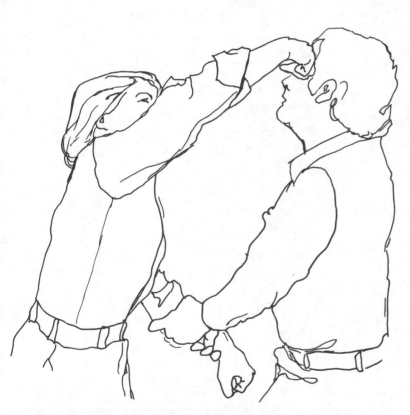

If the attacker's chin is down, shielding his throat, the victim can strike at his temples, followed by a snap kick or a knee to the groin.

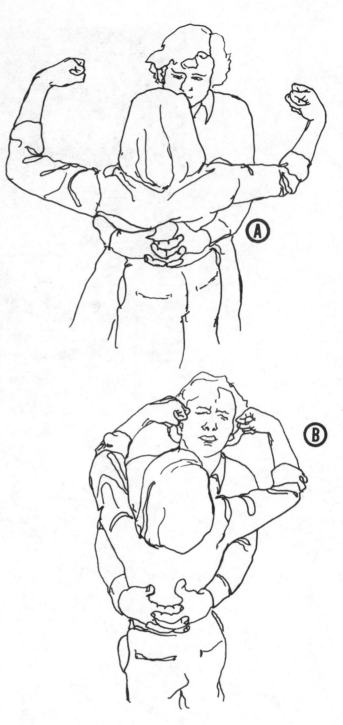

Grasping her around the waist (A), the attacker attempts to drag his victim toward him, to intimidate her and excite himself. Forming the knuckled V with both fists, the victim strikes him on both temples simultaneously (B).

When attacked frontally, the victim can grasp the attacker by the shirt and drive a braced third finger into his windpipe. His air supply is cut off, and he may immediately release her and drop to the ground. Or, she can strike at his temples with the knuckles of both hands.

Top: If the attacker lunges at a seated victim, she should grasp his sleeve and pull him forward, driving her arm straight up between his legs, aiming a crushing blow at the testicles. Below: Here the wrist executes the blow, causing the attacker to topple over her. She can now push him away and seek help. This technique is especially recommended when threatened while seated on a couch or in a car.

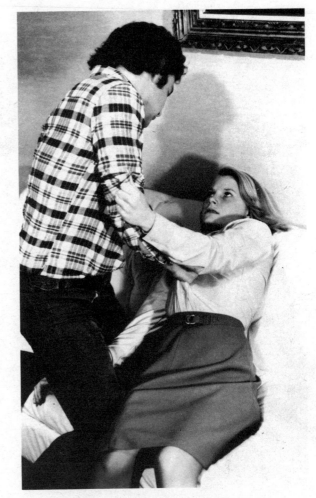

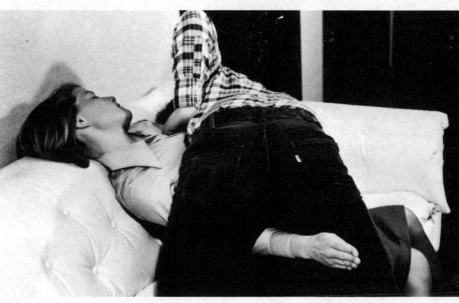

The victim keeps her arm extended and stiff, pounding her attacker's testicles as many times as necessary. She can also grasp the testicles and squeeze them hard, which will cause the attacker to faint from pain.

The victim can use her knee (A) to strike her attacker in the ribs (B) or the kidneys (C).

CHAPTER 6

DEFENSE AGAINST BEING STRIPPED ABOVE THE WAIST

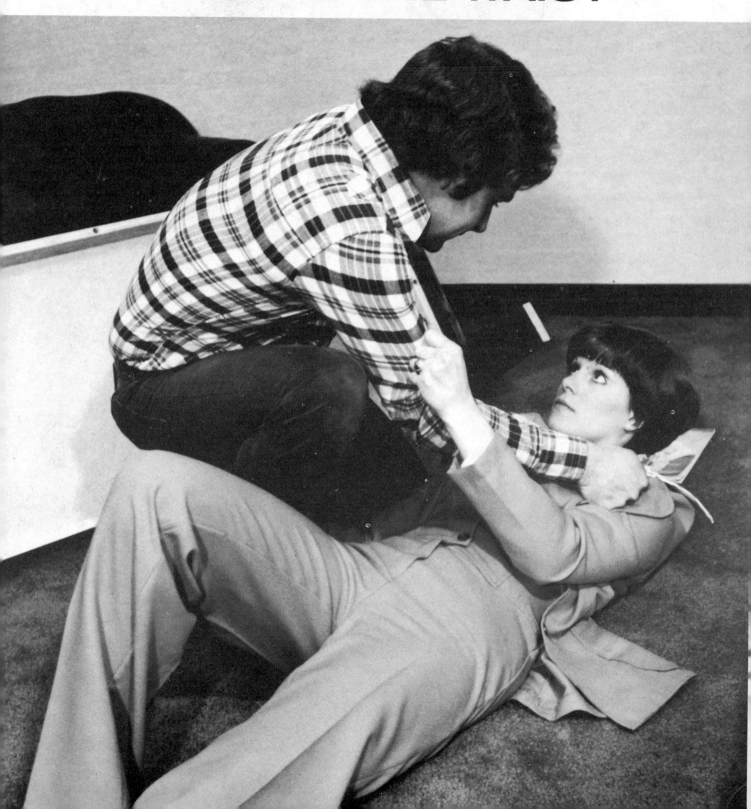

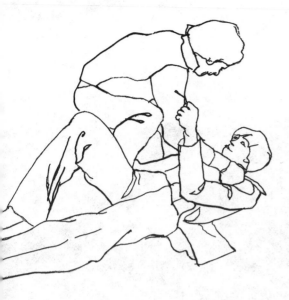

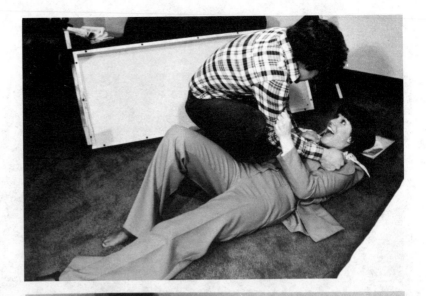

Rape takes time. The attacker must excite himself to achieve an erection and penetration. As he strips the victim above the waist to fondle her and arouse himself, she should grasp him by the sleeve and simultaneously thrust her hand between his legs. While getting into position, she can scream in his face and push him away. When ready to strike, she pulls the attacker forward by the sleeve and drives her hand upward into his testicles.

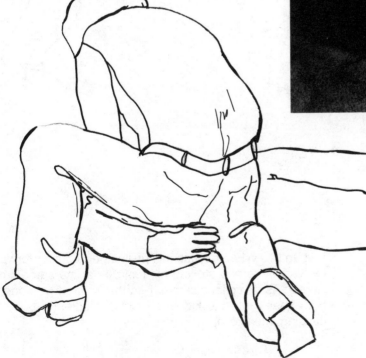

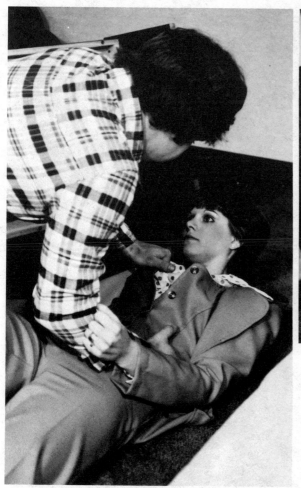

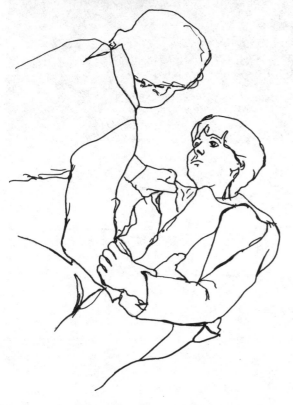

Left: In this view, the victim is pulling her attacker forward by his sleeve and striking his testicles at the same time. Above: As he collapses over her, the victim drives one or both knees into his kidneys or ribs, shattering bone or causing internal injury.

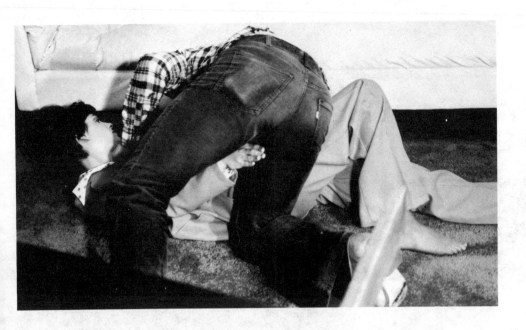

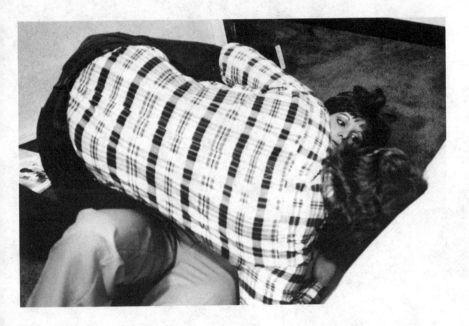

Top: The blade of the hand strikes the testicles. Center: The attacker topples over the victim; now she can also squeeze the testicles. Bottom: If he attempts to rise, the victim can knee him in the kidneys or continue to strike in the groin area. The attacker should be writhing in pain at this point.

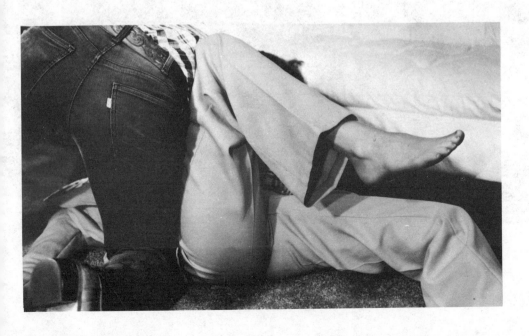

Defense Against Being Stripped Below The Waist

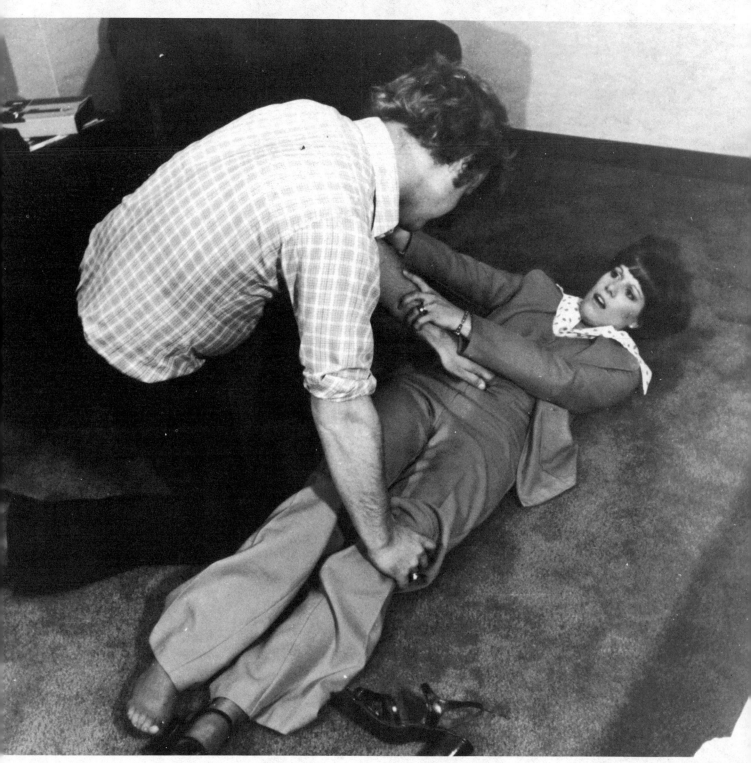

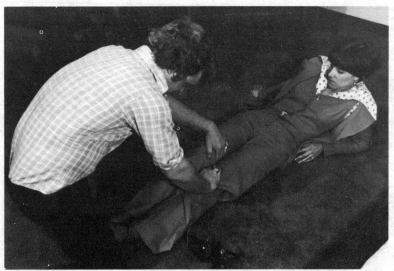

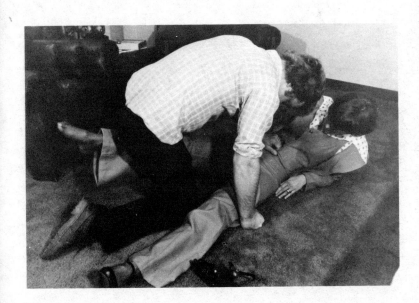

Top: The victim must hold her legs together tightly to force the attacker to try to spread them apart, thus distracting him from the location of her foot. She must be careful not to resist too strongly; he may hit her in the stomach, leaving her breathless and unable to defend herself. Bottom: As he moves forward to strip her, one hand fumbles with her clothing, the other is used to brace himself. The victim should then drive her shinbone directly up between his legs at his testicles, making him collapse on top of her.

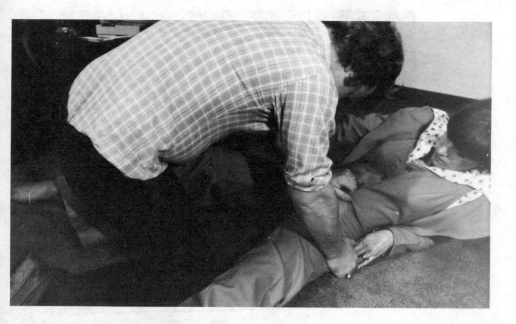

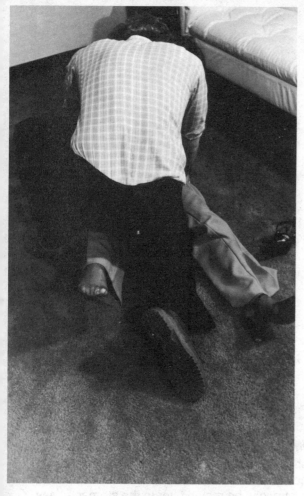

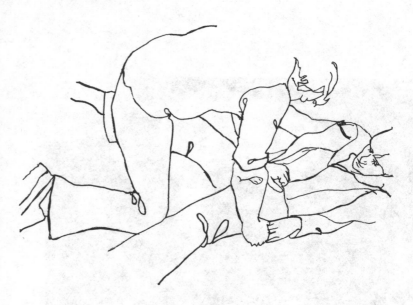

Note the position of the victim's leg. She can repeatedly pound her shinbone into her attacker's testicles. As he topples over her, the victim can slice at his trachea with the blade of her hand, pound his temples with her knuckles, or smash the top of her head against his face. Note the position of the attacker—specifically, where his knee is. He will have to move considerably forward for penetration, and this broadens the target area for the victim.

CHAPTER 7

DEFENSE AGAINST THE CHOKE

The rapist who attacks a woman from the front is far more vulnerable than one who attacks from the rear, and he runs a much greater risk of identification.

The standing straight-arm choke is when the attacker extends his arms and grabs his victim by the throat. This is an amateurish hold, usually not very effective; for in this position it is easy to disturb his balance. The victim should immediately lower her chin and "bow out" by moving away from his thumbs, which have no strength. Simultaneously, she can side-kick him in the groin, kneecap, or side of the leg.

Another method, if taken by surprise, is to lower the chin and press it against the attacker's hands, thus diluting some of the strength of the choke. The victim then grasps the attacker's arms and pulls downward while at the same time snap-kicking at his groin or kneecap, or scraping her foot down the side of his shinbone. She can also suddenly drop to the ground, on both knees, and drive the blade of her hand up between his legs; or grasp his shirt with both hands, smash her head into his face as he pulls back, and drive her knee into his groin.

The close-in choke—when the attacker's arms are bent at the elbows—calls for a similar defense technique. The victim lowers her chin onto the attacker's hands and then strikes at his temples with the knuckles of both of her hands. If he survives this, she knees him in the groin, kicks him in the shin, or stomps his instep. The victim can also grasp him by the shoulders, rocking him up and down, and then follow through with a snap-kick, a knee to the groin, a head smash into his face, or a knuckle punch at the temples. Jabbing stiffened fingers into the flesh below the earlobes or directly into the tracheal tube will cause intense enough pain to effect release. The victim can also poke her index fingers into the sides of the attacker's mouth, thumbs underneath his chin, and drag downward on her hands.

The order of movements is not important; any of these techniques properly executed, can render the attacker impotent. The important point to remember is to lower the chin as quickly as possible to slacken the grip on the throat so the victim's oxygen supply is not cut off.

The collar choke, taught in the armed forces and as a martial art, is more difficult to break but, fortunately, seldom used. Here the attacker places one arm around the victim's throat, using wrist or forearm to exert pressure on the windpipe while pulling down on her collar or blouse from the back, causing almost immediate loss of consciousness. The victim must turn her head to the side; dragging away from the choke will only increase the pressure. The victim grabs the sleeve of the arm pulling her shirt and tries to push in the opposite direction. If he is pulling downward, she pulls upward. With her free hand, she punches her knuckles at his temples or eyes, or tries to snap-kick or knee him in the groin or shin.

When forced down on her back, with the attacker on top and trying to choke her, the victim can push her chin forward and pound her knuckles at his temples. If this is impossible, she can grasp his shirt with two hands and push in the opposite direction with both arms, then attempt to knee him in the spine from the rear. If she can arch her pelvis, the victim can bring him forward, enabling her to strike at the groin or to squeeze his testicles.

If the attacker's arms are bent as he tries to choke her, the victim can jab her fingernails into the flesh below the earlobes and press straight up, lacerating the skin. Then she can strike him in the temples with her knuckles, and at the same time arch her body to knee him in the groin or kick him in the shinbone. At this point, the assailant, fallen away, can be chopped or squeezed in the testicles.

If pinned to the ground with her arms held down, the victim can startle her attacker by screaming "KIAI!" and strike his face with her forehead. Then she can raise her pelvis and knees and hit him in the back, sending him flying over her head. If the victim is straddled with one leg, she can drive her own leg into his groin, which will break his grip and free her hands. A pinned victim cannot be raped; the attacker must use his hands to help penetration. However, in this position he can also drive a knee into the victim's stomach, knocking the breath out of her and shattering her control. Fortunately, this doesn't often happen, and if the victim can keep her head, she will have the opportunity to take defensive action.

When gripped in a choke from the front, the victim lowers her chin onto her attacker's hands and drops immediately to the ground. The attacker has to bend to drag her up, exposing his crotch as a target, and she can then drive the blade of her hand straight up into his testicles—or she can squeeze the testicles. The victim continues by leaping to her feet—grasping his shirt for leverage—and driving a knee into his groin. If he is still functioning, she can follow up with any of the defensive techniques previously discussed.

Again the victim drops her jaw onto her attacker's hands to ease the pressure of the frontal choke. This attacker stands close with his arms bent, so the victim grasps his sleeves at the elbows and literally rocks him, pulling down and pushing up. As she pumps her arms, she keeps her head down and brings her foot back into a snap-kick position. Then, still gripping his sleeves to steady herself, she extends her leg beyond his groin and drives her shinbone upward to crush his testicles.

An attacker has no strength in his thumbs, so the victim can use her body against them to free herself. She steps backward with one foot, turning it to the side (the left, in these photographs), and drops down under the choking grip, using the weight of her body against the attacker's thumbs. This technique, known as "bowing out," is simple to use and even more effective when accompanied by a harrowing scream of "KIAI!" Once she has bowed out from her crouching position the victim can grip her attacker's belt or shirt and come up strongly with the side of her foot against his knee, or scrape his shinbone and stomp his instep, followed with a snap-kick or a knee to the groin.

In this example, the victim has both hands at her sides. She immediately drops her chin onto her attacker's hand, grasps the arm closest to her chin, and drives her foot into the side of his kneecap, or kicks powerfully at his instep. To follow up, she drops to the ground, extends a stiffened arm through his groin, and smashes upward, the forearm crushing the testicles. She can repeat this blow as often as necessary. From this position, the victim can also butt the top of her head into the attacker's face or drive a knee into his groin.

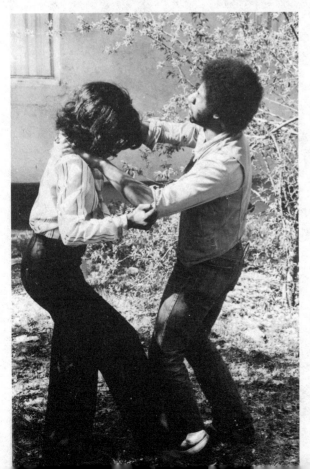

When thrown to the ground and in danger of being choked, the victim should grasp her attacker's shirt sleeves, push away, and bring her chin forward. This will ease the pressure in her throat. Next, raising the pelvic region, including the hips, drive both knees into the attacker's buttocks and spine, while at the same time pulling down and forward on his sleeves. Losing his balance, the attacker should fall straight forward, directly on his head.

Once the rapist has fallen on his head, the victim continues to hold his sleeves and knees him in the testicles. She can even reach down and squeeze the testicles to inflict more intense and disabling pain. Or, the victim can roll the attacker off and strike the blade of her hand against his windpipe or the bridge of his nose.

CHAPTER 8

DEFENSE AGAINST RAPE WHEN FACE-DOWN

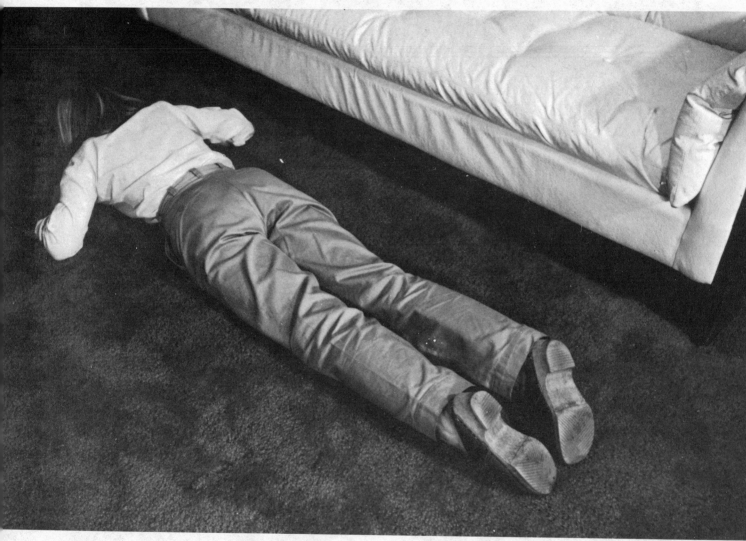

Most rapists prefer to penetrate their victims from the rear, with the woman lying face down on the floor or bed as shown above. That way, later identification will be more difficult for the victim when reporting the crime to police, since she was unable to look at the rapist during the act itself.

It is necessary, therefore, to devise special techniques with which to extricate oneself from this difficult position. The victim's best weapon in this case is the back of her head, which can inflict great pain and injury to the rapist's more vulnerable forehead, nose, and mouth areas.

The victim simulates grasping the attacker's collar and attempts to dislodge him by pushing against him while at the same time she draws one leg upward to facilitate less painful penetration.

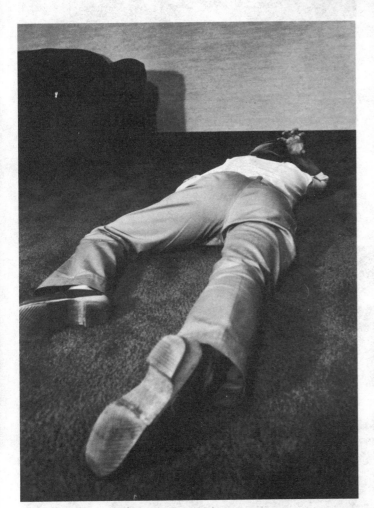 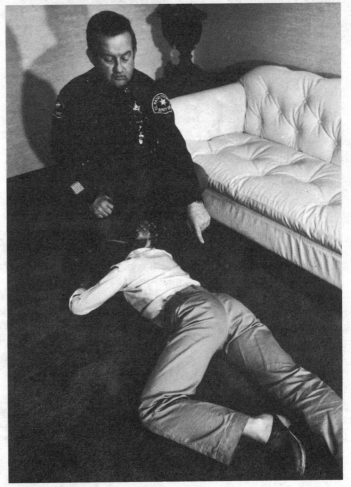

Still gripping the attacker, she smashes her head back into his face. (At such close range, she may be able to fracture his nose.) The next move is to snap the bent leg straight, preventing the attacker from withdrawing and putting pressure on the penis while causing the testicles to be stretched too far. This will cause the victim some discomfort but also cause agonizing pain to the rapist. The victim can then extricate herself and continue the defense, striking him in the throat or groin.

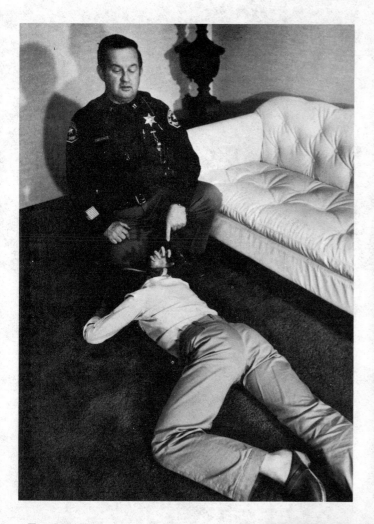

Top left: The victim grabs the attacker about the head or collar, pushes against him, and prepares for the next move. Top right: She smashes her head back into his face. Right: The leg is snapped straight. The victim can now free herself to strike again if necessary or to seek help.

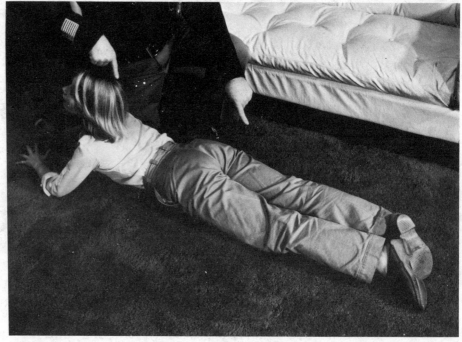

Alternate Defense On The Ground

When thrown to the ground, with the attacker on top, the previously outlined bedroom technique should be used. Grasping the sleeve of one arm or the arm itself, the victim raises the opposite leg and snaps it over, dislodging her attacker so she can roll over to use the blade of her hand, a spear hand, or even her fist against his throat. The blade of the hand is usually most effective. To follow up, she can knee him in the groin or crush his testicles with her hand. A 300-lb. attacker can be disabled with this technique.

When pinned with her back to the ground, the victim raises her pelvis and drives both knees into her attacker's buttocks, sending him sprawling over her head.

Left: The victim's knees strike the buttocks and spine of the attacker. Since both his hands are gripping the victim, there is no way the attacker can retain his balance; he must topple forward over her head. If there is enough room, this same technique can be used on a bed, on a couch, or on the car seat.

Above, the assailant lands on his head, perhaps injuring himself on impact. But to insure his complete disability, the victim should reach out and squeeze his testicles. A man will lose consciousness in about seven-tenths of a second when his testicles are crushed.

Above: If the attempt on the testicles is ineffective, or the attacker has landed with his throat exposed, the victim can drive the blade of her hand across his tracheal tube. A combination of both techniques can be used.

CHAPTER 9

TYPICAL RAPE SITES

In Hallways

As the photographs on this page indicate so graphic-ally, hallways and other small, constricted areas make ideal settings for the rapist. Elevators, automobiles, garages, basements, bathrooms and bedrooms are other typical rape sites.

In the first photo, the victim has been grabbed from behind (this is the rapist's favorite technique, as we shall see) in a darkened hallway of an apartment build-ing. Note that she is holding her apartment door keys in her right hand — that same key can often be used (see Ch. 10) as an extremely effective defensive wea-pon. In this instance, though, the victim is forced to drop the keys and use her arms to ward off the attacker (second photo). Notice that she has turned her head to the left to avoid being choked; at the same time, she

has grabbed the man's right hand in hers and stepped forward with her right foot. This gives her the proper leverage and freedom to deliver a crippling blow (third photo) to her attacker's testicles. She does this by driving her free left arm down and up, a motion similar to that used in the golf swing. This blow, especially when it is repeated several times in quick succession, should leave the assailant totally disabled and give the woman time to escape.

In the pages to follow, we will show how to defend yourself in an elevator, against a wall, in the bedroom, and in (and out of) a car. You are urged to learn these techniques, practice them with a friend or relative, and repeat them until they become automatic responses in case of emergency.

Defense Against Attack in an Elevator

The elevator in a commercial building, during the early morning or late evening hours when traffic is sparse, is a prime staging area for assault. In this photograph, the victim is being overpowered and dragged into an elevator, which the attacker can then stop between floors or immobilize by cutting off the power.

Although struggling in a small area—and probably terrorized—the victim can still defend herself easily, especially before the elevator doors have closed, using any of the techniques in this book. But if she is dragged into the elevator—then what? She must be at least partially disrobed for actual penetration, whether in a standing position or on the floor, whether face-down or face-up. Even in the brief time it takes for this, she can strike her attacker's eyes, back, or kidneys, using her head, knee, blade of her hand, or knuckles. Once her attacker is disabled—or momentarily stopped—she must immediately hit the elevator alarm button. Many elevators are equipped with telephones; the victim can summon help this way and then move the car to a floor for exit. The victim must always attempt to remain cool and controlled.

The best defense against rape is a companion, the second best is alertness. When boarding an elevator alone at night a woman should carry her keys or a rolled-up magazine in her hand. But remember—not all other passengers are potential rapists.

Taken from behind, the victim immediately turns her head to the attacker's upper arm (A). Then she hurls her head back, striking the rapist on the bridge of the nose (B) or elsewhere on the face.

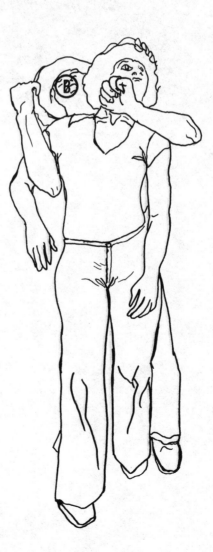

81

In this side view, the attacker has been struck in the face by the victim's head (A), but he has not released his hold. The victim extends her fist, palm up (B), and pivots her feet (C) for the next retaliatory move.

The attacker—again struck—clutches his stomach. The victim, fist drawn back, is ready to deliver a blow to the attacker's throat. Or, as in the photographs below, the victim can strike at the rapist's groin with her arm.

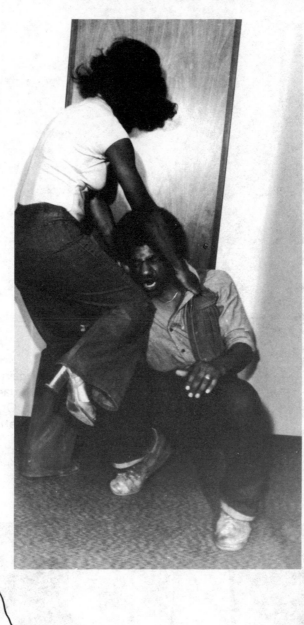

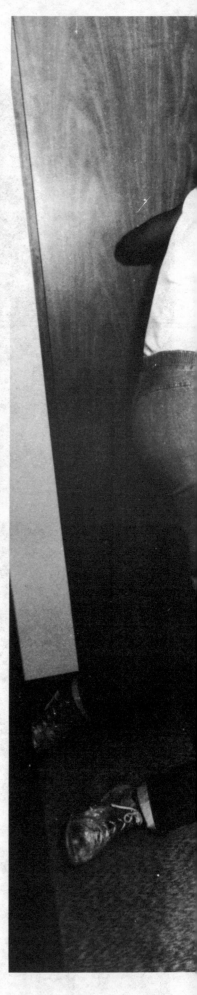

If the attacker has fallen but is still a threat, the victim can grasp any part of his clothing (A) and knee him hard in the face (B), bringing her foot into position to snap-kick him in the testicles (C). This should be sufficient to render him harmless or unconscious.

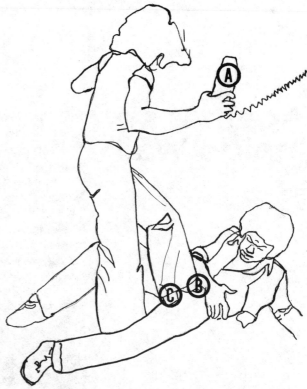

Even an elevator telephone (A) can be used as a weapon for striking the fallen attacker on the head or in the throat. The victim can also stomp the rapist in the groin with her whole foot (B) or a sharp heel (C) or hit any other vulnerable body area.

Against an Inside Wall

This photograph illustrates a hold commonly used by rapists. Notice how the victim's hand is gripped from behind and pressed against the wall, her legs immobilized by pressure from the assailant's leg. The manipulation of the breast is frequently employed as an attempt at mutual excitement and to initiate involuntary secretions before the victim's clothing is stripped away and penetration takes place. This may last anywhere from five to twenty minutes and is often called "the stage of possession." It is also a stage during which male gullibility may be employed in the victim's own defense.

While the attacker is caressing the victim, attempting to stimulate her as well as himself, the victim can take advantage of his gullibility by saying things like, "Kiss me," or "I'm afraid . . . I'll do whatever you want me to." When the attacker leans forward to kiss her, the victim brings her head back (A) and then suddenly forward, driving her forehead into the attacker's face (B). This may fracture the attacker's nose or bruise his face; it should cause sufficient pain for him to release his grasp.

Right: As the rapist holds his face in pain, the victim should drop suddenly to the floor, bringing her hand back as far as she can. Below: Retaining a grip on the attacker, she drives her hand or arm straight up into his groin, repeating the action as often as necessary. At this point, with facial injuries and crushed testicles, the assailant should be rendered harmless.

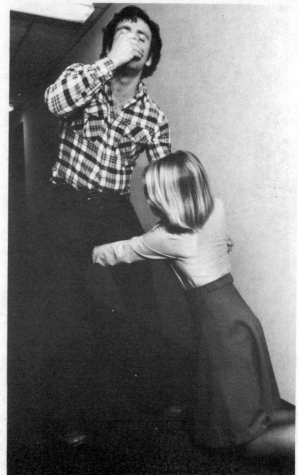

88

The victim should immediately stand, shape her knuckles into a "V" fist (left), and thrust it powerfully into the attacker's throat (below). A blow of this sort can crush the trachea, even cause a fatal injury. A snap kick to the groin can follow, but with facial, testicle, and throat injuries, the attacker should be helpless by now. If the assailant is too tall for any of these methods, the victim can scream suddenly and then drop limply to the floor. As he drags her back up, the blade of her hand should be between his legs, ready to drive up at his groin. This is called the "using-your-head" technique of defense, again playing on the attacker's gullibility.

89

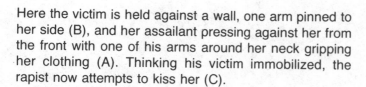

Here the victim is held against a wall, one arm pinned to her side (B), and her assailant pressing against her from the front with one of his arms around her neck gripping her clothing (A). Thinking his victim immobilized, the rapist now attempts to kiss her (C).

With all her strength, the victim drives the top of her head into the assailant's face, at the same time screaming as loudly as she can. She can repeat this action as often as she is able, perhaps fracturing his nose or at least causing him debilitating pain.

Top left: A close view of the victim's head striking the attacker's face. The victim should keep her body straight so she can readily deliver another blow. The attacker, in his pain, may push her away; to strike him again she must move back into position.

Bottom left: If another blow is unnecessary, the victim should instantly drop to the ground. The attacker may still be gripping her collar, but she is now in a position to defend herself.

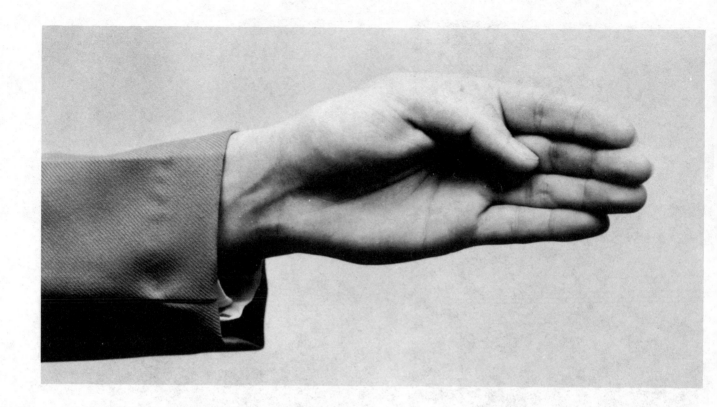

It is not necessary to be a karate expert or to practice beating boards to condition the hand for striking power. But it is important to remember to turn down the thumb in order not to dislocate it, as illustrated above. The fingers must be held tightly together — especially the index and little fingers — and pressed against the two middle fingers. Hold one hand out, thumb up, in front of you, and strike the palm of your other hand. Then bring the thumb down and hit the other palm again; you will feel your additional power immediately. Now assume the thumb-down position once more, first and little fingers tightened, and strike with the bottom of the hand to which the thumb is pointing. The area from the wrist to the little finger (below), in combination with the wrist itself and the forearm, can be utilized as a deadly weapon without much practice. Be sure to learn the position with both left and right hands.

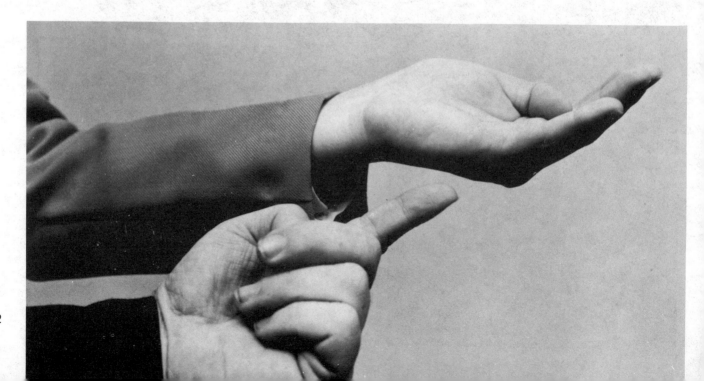

Keeping one knee on the ground for balance, the victim extends her hand between the attacker's legs and powerfully chops straight up (A). Drawing back her hand, the victim can also squeeze the testicles, causing agonizing pain and even unconsciousness. If necessary, the victim can strike more than once.

When attacked frontally with her buttocks against the wall (A), the victim should place her hands on the assailant's upper arms.

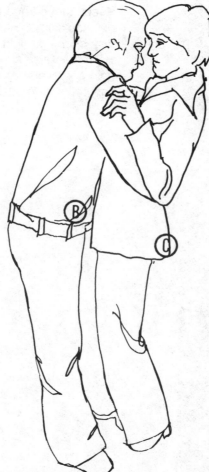

Next, she thrusts her pelvis directly at the assailant (B)—this pleases him but also creates space between the victim and the wall (C). Moving him back and forth, the victim plays on the assailant's gullibility, asking him to kiss her, hold her close, move faster, while maneuvering him directly in front of her.

When the attacker is directly in front of her, the victim should smash her forehead into his face, while at the same time pushing him away from her.

The forehead, which is broad, can be struck against the bridge of the nose or the mouth, or against both in a quick succession of blows, to cause extreme pain to the assailant.

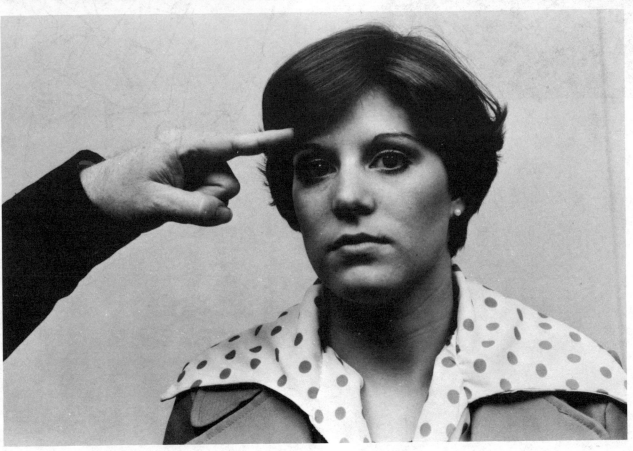

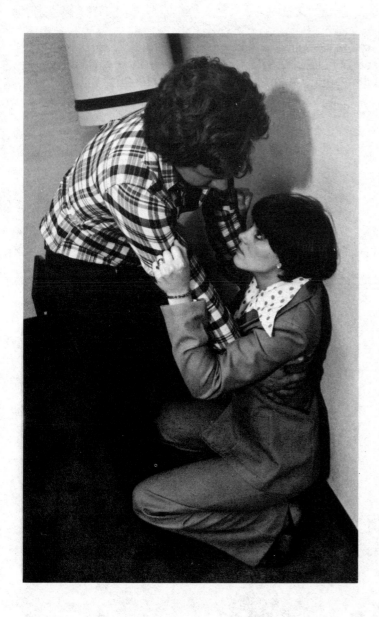

After striking the attacker with her head, the victim should immediately fall to her knees. If the assailant is gripping the victim beneath the armpits, it may be more difficult to strike with the hand between the legs. In this case, the victim should try to stay on the balls of her feet, still holding to the assailant's shirtsleeves (A and B). Using his clothing as leverage, the victim can then drive one knee directly up into his testicles, disabling him with pain (C).

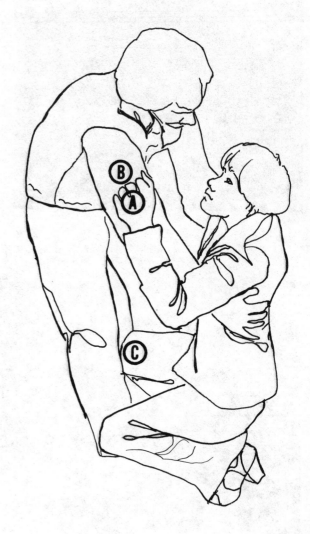

Following the preceding move, the victim knees the rapist in the testicles (A) while maintaining her grip on his shirtsleeves. She can then use the top of her head to butt him (B), or knee him again if she is still in danger.

This is the part of the knee which causes the greatest damage to the testicles, especially when used while firmly gripping the assailant's sleeves, arms, or belt for leverage.

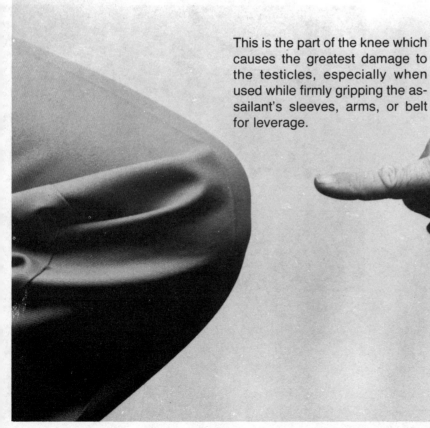

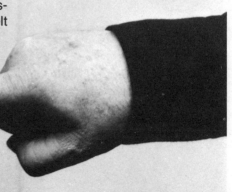

In the Bedroom

One of the most traumatic experiences for a woman is to be suddenly awakened in her bedroom, by a rapist. To stifle any scream which might alert the neighbors, the assailant will advance toward the bed and cram his hand or a pillow over the victim's mouth. Before he reaches her, the victim can use her knuckles or knee for a blow to the attacker's kidneys or try a snap kick into his groin area. If possible, she should scream, "Fire!" If one hand is free, the victim can pick up a bedside telephone or ashtray and strike at the assailant's temples. She can then use her knee or knuckles to hit out at his eyes, throat, or any vulnerable areas.

Suppose the victim, in her shock, has allowed that interval to slip away and the rapist has overpowered her. If at all possible, she can attempt to placate him, assure him of her cooperation. He will then attempt to disrobe her and touch her intimately. Again, if she can manage, the victim should try to reassure the attacker, promising willingness. He will then probably move to her stomach or breasts in an attempt at mutual excitement. At this point, the victim can thrust up her knee in a tremendous driving blow at his temple—which could knock him out, fracture his skull, or, in some cases, even kill him. At this stage, any available weapon can be used—knuckles, telephone, ballpoint pen, or keys— even the victim's head butting the rapist in the face.

But if the victim is still imprisoned by the rapist, she can pretend to move to his rhythm (he must become aroused before penetration) and at this point he may be off guard. Now she can grip one sleeve or the flesh beside one elbow, raise the opposite leg, and pull him over and off her. (With this method, it is possible to throw as much as 300 lbs. of dead weight from a bed, even more when on the floor.) Once free, the victim can roll over and strike at the assailant's throat with the blade of her hand, or drive her knee into his groin. Here again, the victim can hurl her own head at the rapist's face, causing brutal injury.

Sometimes when a woman startles a burglar in her bedroom, he may throw her on the bed and attempt to rape her. The techniques outlined above should be employed, and a victim should always remember to *scream* and to *move,* penetration under duress is extremely difficult. And she should always place a potential weapon by her bed—not a gun or a knife, but a set of keys, a magazine, a ballpoint pen, the telephone itself. Remember, too, it *is* possible to dislodge a man from a bed—and even overpower him.

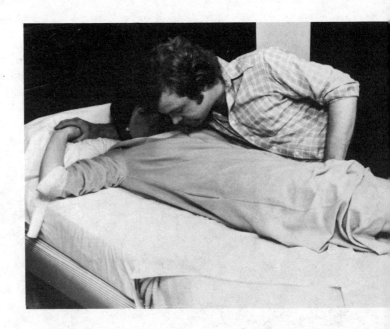

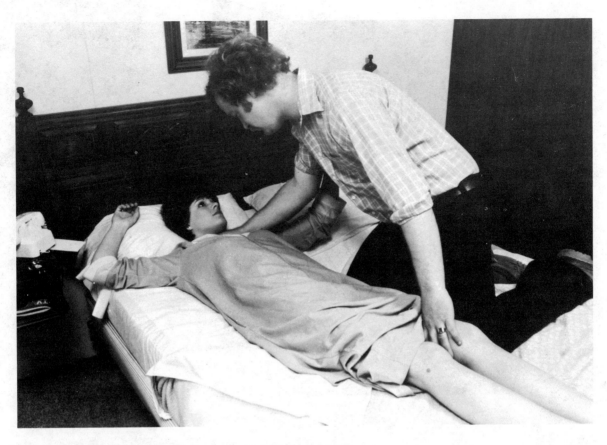

The assailant will eventually become lost in his own excitement. Because he feels she is willing, he will remove his hand from the victim's throat but maintain a grip on her with his arm or hand.

The victim should tell the assailant that she is frightened but that she will cooperate with him. In the photograph, he is caressing her but keeping a cautionary hand on her throat despite her assurances. At this point, she would probably be stripped.

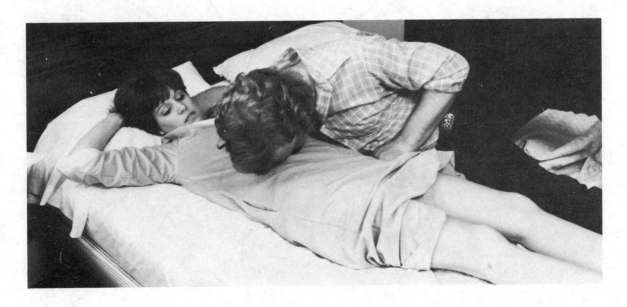

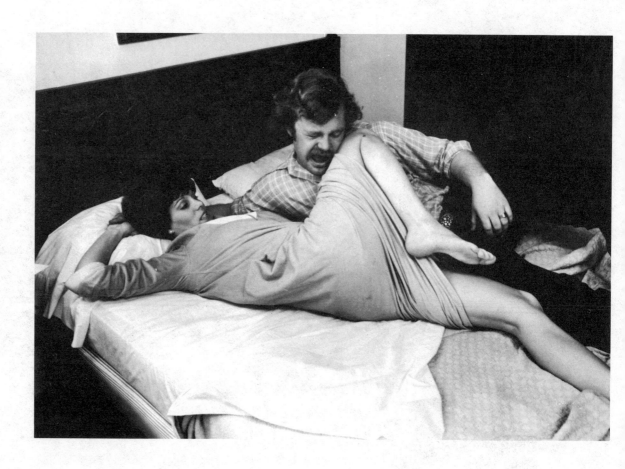

The rapist's head, when bent over the front of the victim's body, is exposed to counterattack. The victim can drive her knee into the assailant's temple, causing a fracture if sufficient power is brought to the blow.

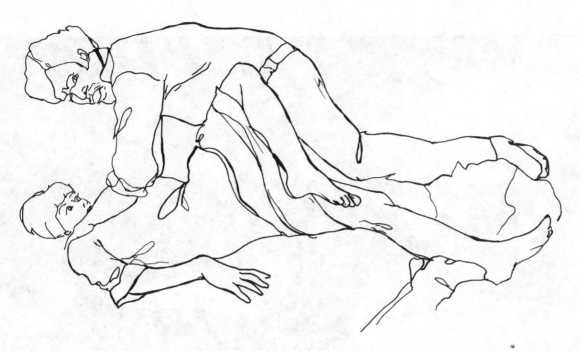

Even if the rapist has the victim by the throat, she can still knee him in the kidneys, using some of the previous techniques as a follow-up. Any situation can be met with ingenuity if the victim remains calm. Most rape attacks occur in the dark, and the victim can often play on male gullibility to defeat her attacker. By assuring him of her fear and cooperation, she can lull him into a state of confidence. Once he is lost in the effort of mutual stimulation, the victim's own body is her best weapon, along with the adrenalin that gives her extra strength. In this case, a well-placed blow from the knee can cause the assailant serious injury.

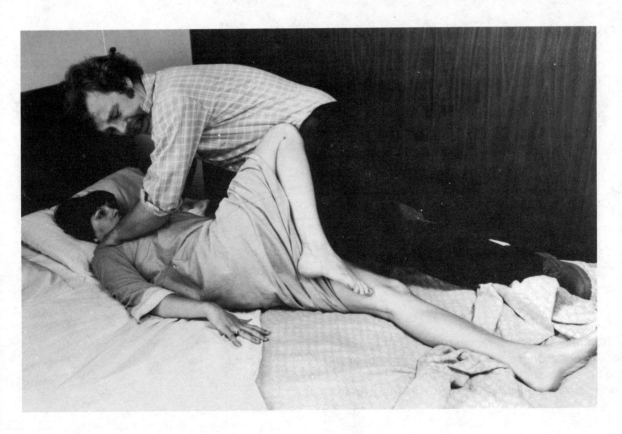

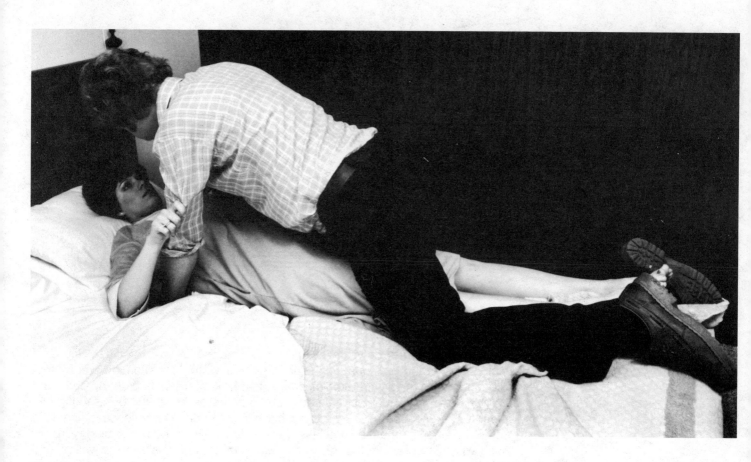

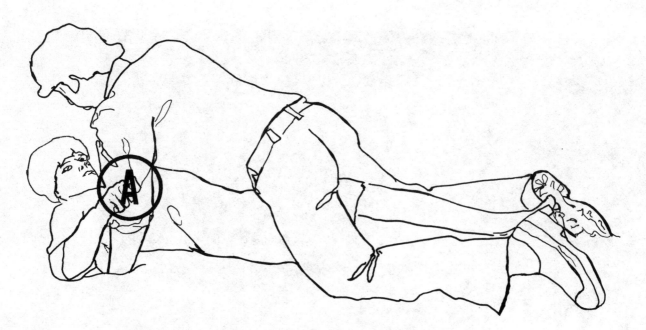

If the victim gives herself time to think, she can use the rapist's own actions to defeat him. Before penetration, he will often try to frighten as well as arouse her. The victim should grasp his shirt (A), arch her body, and begin to move with him, reassuring him and using his gullibility to excite him into carelessness.

This photograph and diagram show how, by grasping the attacker's clothing, hair, or flesh and suddenly raising the opposite leg (B), the victim can dislodge the attacker. Even a person of slight build can throw off an attacker weighing 300 lbs. or more using this technique. It is, however, most successful when the victim is forced down onto a bed or couch.

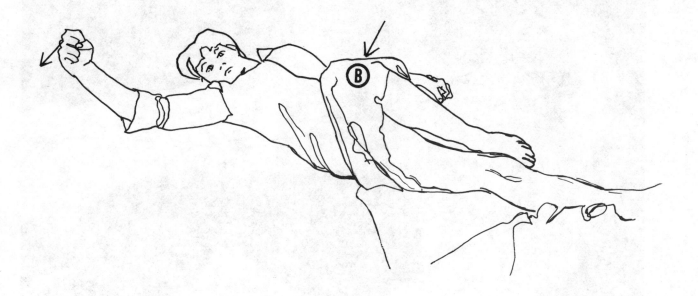

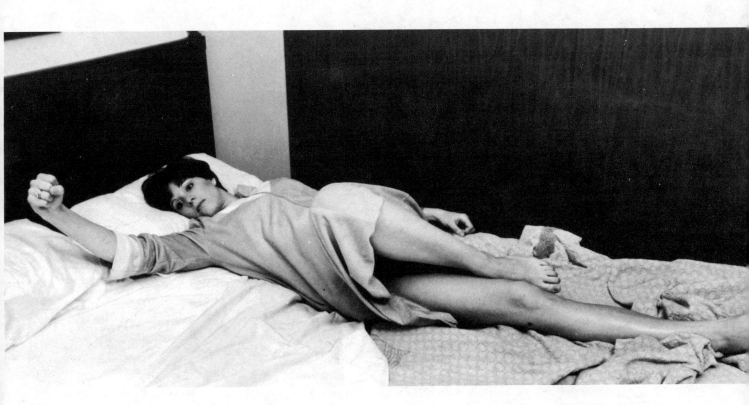

After throwing the assailant to the side, the victim can drive the blade of her hand across his trachea or her knee into his testicles (B). (This is especially effective if the attacker has removed his clothing.)

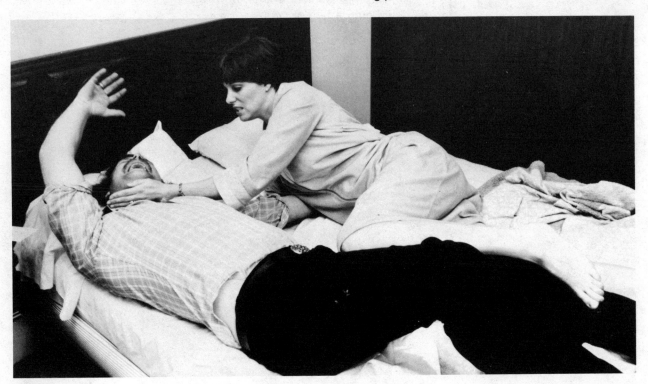

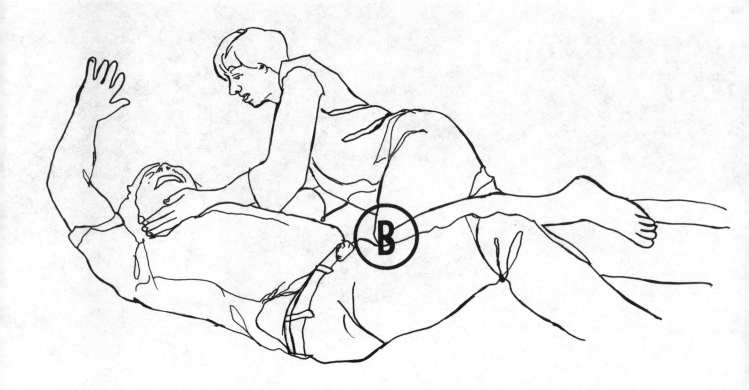

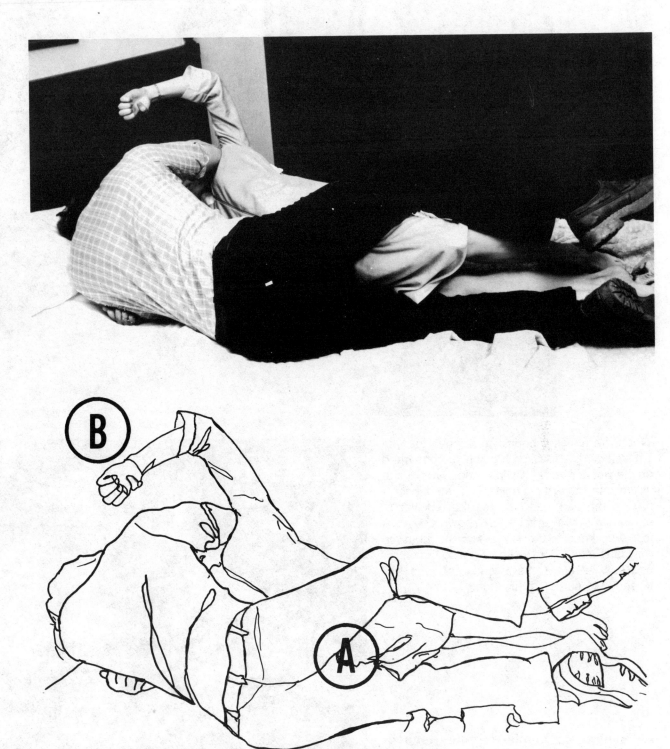

Though still on his side, the attacker may try to hold the victim down by throwing his leg over hers (A). This exposes his testicles to a blow from the victim's knee. Because the victim is fighting him, the attacker may try to choke the victim. Should this happen, use the blade of the hand or the knuckles (B) and drive them into the attacker's temples. Continue hitting him in the groin and on the temples until he loses consciousness or is fought off. Throughout this book we suggest screaming "KIAI!" into the attacker's face; this will serve to give you added strength and courage and may dismay the attacker.

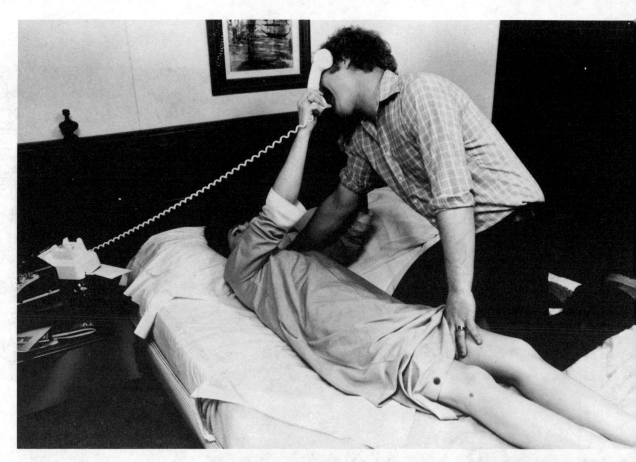

When the attacker begins to remove the victim's clothing, he will probably place one hand on the victim's throat. By lowering her chin, the victim can ease the choke. If a telephone is next to the bed, she can use the receiver to strike him in the temples, as shown above. A follow-up knee to the kidneys or the stomach will disable him. The victim can also punch repeatedly at the rapist's ears and use her forehead to smash at his face.

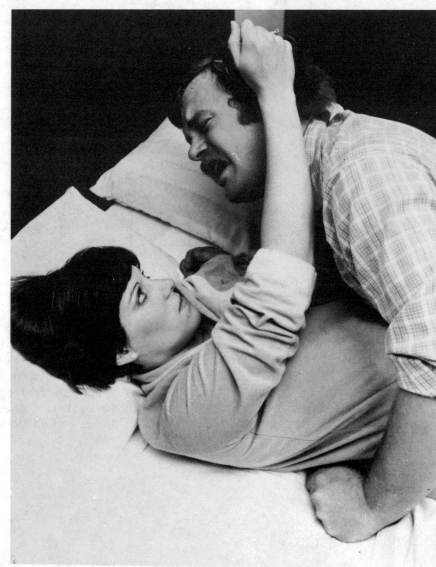

An ashtray is another useful weapon. Clutched in the victim's hand, it is difficult to pry loose, and she can reach down with it to strike at her assailant's groin. Dangerous weapons—such as a gun or tear gas—should *not* be kept in the room; they can easily be turned against a victim. Common objects—keys, a pen, a matchbook, a magazine—contribute to effective and unexpected defense.

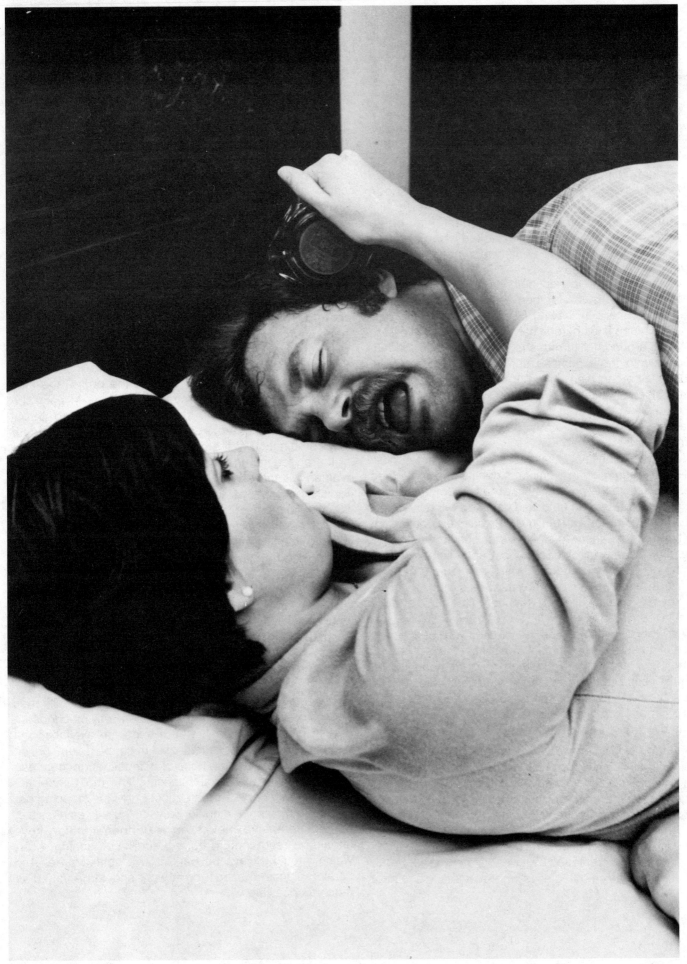

In the Car

A woman has several ways to protect herself from being attacked inside or outside her car. One is to avoid the common error of not having the car keys in her hand when walking toward her automobile. A woman is very vulnerable when standing at her car door, searching her purse for her keys. A key is an effective weapon, even more than a gun or knife. (This should also be done to prevent being attacked when entering a house or apartment. Women should make a habit of having their keys ready.)

Another way is to inspect both the front and back seats before entering the car, for there are ways of breaking into even locked cars. If, having failed to look into the back seat, a woman finds herself behind the wheel with an arm wrapped around her throat, she should turn her head immediately to the attacker's upper arm, to avoid being choked. She can then drive her key into the back of his hand, which should make him drop his arm in pain. Next, she can either leap from the vehicle or turn and strike her attacker's face, using many of the techniques discussed in this chapter.

A woman alone in a car faces other dangers. While halted at a stop sign in a quiet residential or remote area, there is always the possibility of an attacker jumping into the vehicle through an unlocked door or a window. In this situation, a woman should pull her car keys out of the ignition and use them to strike at her attacker's temples, eyes, forehead, windpipe, or hand, depending on the positions of victim and attacker. This technique is most effective at night because of the attacker's inability to see the keys; it can also be used when more than one attacker is involved.

If a woman, while driving, becomes aware of the presence of an attacker in the back seat of her car, she should try to blow her horn to summon help, or head for the nearest police station or even a lighted gas station. Unfortunately, in most cases, she is powerless to do so, and even if her horn alerted passersby, she would be far away by the time police arrived.

The rape whistle provides a distinctive call for help and is used mainly on college campuses and other areas where its special sound is a familiar alarm. Unfortunately, it has not proved effective in congested localities where attacks take place frequently during both day and night. The rape whistle is useful only when people have been trained to its sound; the general public is unfamiliar with it.

If a woman is threatened by a weapon held at her head, she has little choice but to drive wherever she is directed.

She can try to attract attention by turning off her headlights while driving through a congested area, or attempt to jump from the car—even when it is moving—if she has the opportunity. She can even deliberately ram another car or an obstacle.

If unable to accomplish any of these ploys, and facing the attacker now in a parked car, she can try to lower his defenses, assuring him of her cooperation, telling him that she will not resist, and even suggesting oral sex as a beginning. This will give her an opportunity to drop her head and block his vision. Then, either with her car keys or the blade of her hand, she can smash her attacker in the groin area. The victim should try to be sure that her hand is under his knee so that she can follow the contour of his leg, allowing her to strike directly at the testicles and cause the rapist the greatest amount of pain. If she strikes him above the testicles, or even in the penis, she may only stun him. When the attacker doubles in pain, the victim can follow up with blows to the temples or throat with her car keys, her knuckles, the blade of her hand, or any combination of them.

If dragged into the cramped back seat of a vehicle, the woman will more than likely be thrown on her back, the rapist's head above her face. She has the option of striking at his groin or his nerve centers (earlobe, mouth, windpipe, etc.) using her hand or, if she has managed to cling to them, her keys.

If a man forces himself onto a woman who is driving, she can stamp on the brake, throw the car into park or neutral, pull her keys from the ignition, and strike out at her attacker with them. It is also advisable to have a second set of keys in the dashboard area in the event of assault. Another weapon is to scream the phrases "KIAI!" and "SUT!" which forces the air from the lungs, eases fear, and gives additional strength to strike—and might frighten an assailant from the scene.

In some areas of the country, over one half of all rapes occur in vehicles, and there has been a tremendous increase of rapes in vans, where beds are available and consumption of drugs and alcohol might be a contributing factor. However, the methods of defense taught here can be used under any circumstances. The most important factor is *practice*. A woman should practice stopping her car and removing her ignition keys as quickly as possible, testing defensive moves on a partner. Ignition keys should be ready and in hand before approaching a car, which should always be parked in a lighted area. And parking places at school or at work should be varied as much as possible.

A woman should always enter her car quickly and drive confidently away, without turning to a bystander (as in the photograph below). An inquiring look can be misconstrued. If, as in lower right, an attacker forces entry, she must step on the brake immediately and stop the car.

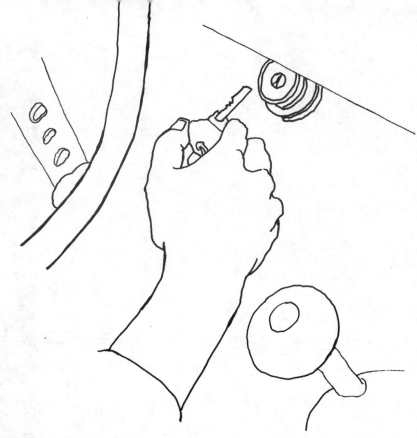

Above: Once the car is stopped, the victim pulls the keys from the ignition. Below: As the attacker reaches out for her, the victim moves the keys into position—point forward with the base against her palm for additional striking power. If the attack occurs at night, the rapist may be unaware that his victim has a weapon.

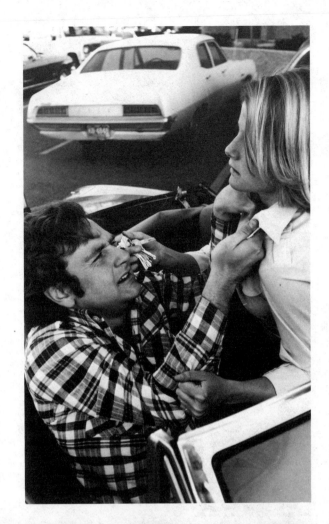

Top right: The attacker has the victim by the throat, pulling her toward him. Bottom right: She should immediately thrust the key into his eye (A) while gripping his shirt to ease the pressure of his hands (B). The victim can drive the key into his eye repeatedly; only a 6-inch blow is needed to inflict a fatal injury.

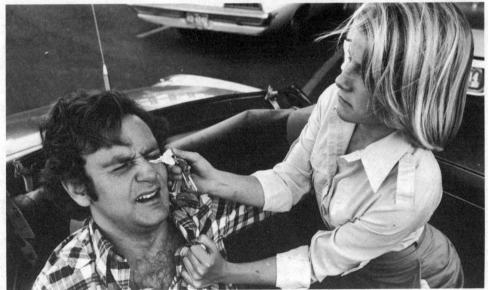

111

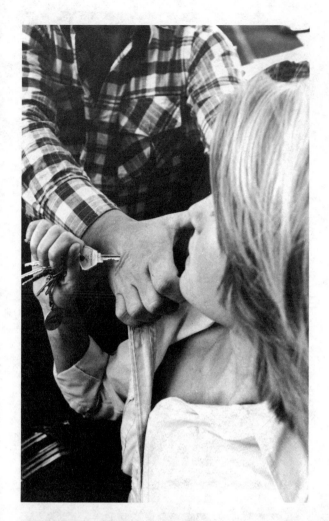

If the attacker approaches the victim from the side, ripping away her clothing or pulling her toward him, the victim can drive the key into the back of his hand, causing overwhelming pain and possibly breaking the small bones. Or, as in the photograph below, she can jab the key into his neck or windpipe.

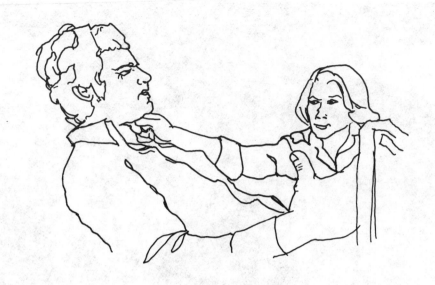

A key driven into the windpipe and then pushed down-ward can cut off all air and cause unconsciousness. A key driven in and held can be fatal.

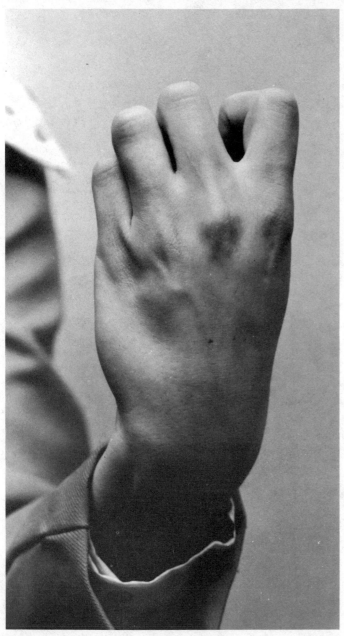

The back seat of a car leaves neither the rapist nor the victim much room for movement. Forced into a corner, where the rapist attempts to strip her, the victim can scream "KIAI!" into his face and grip his shirt as he forces her onto her back. At this point the victim can use the V hand, illustrated in the photograph at left. Palm facing inward, the first and second fingers forming a V shape. With the hand in this—or in the clenched knuckles—position, the victim can strike at her assailant's windpipe, the bridge of his nose, or the area between his eyes, causing intense pain and damage.

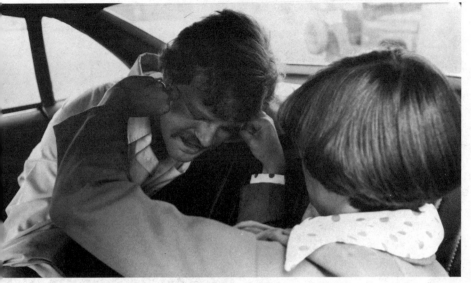

A weaponless victim *can* fight back. In cramped quarters and at the attacker's mercy, the victim can tell him she is frightened and that she will cooperate— and then smash the knuckles of both hands into his temples or grab his collar and drive her head into his face. If he is attempting to remove her clothing below the waist, the victim can bring her knee up and strike him in the temples or can use her "V" hand to punch him in the windpipe. Once he is incapacitated, the victim can leap from the car.

An unprepared woman can be easily over-powered and dragged into any vehicle. But common sense can extricate a victim from the most difficult situations. Always have the car keys (house and apartment, too) ready; whenever possible, walk with someone, avoid unlighted areas, and park as close to a desti-nation as can be managed. Preparation and practice of self-defense techniques are all-important for protection against rape.

Grasp the key tightly, either at the base of the palm or against the other keys to achieve the greatest power when striking a blow. Aim the point of the key at the back of the assailant's hand, a sensitive area (B).

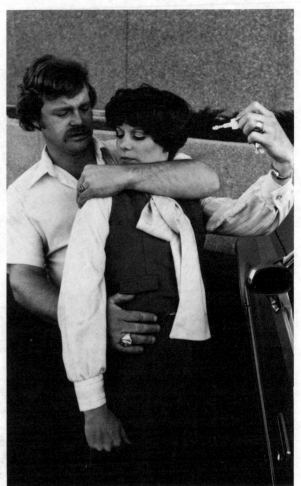

By striking the back of the hand with the point of the key (B), the victim can often obtain immediate release. If the key penetrates the flesh with enough force, it may fracture some small bones, rendering the assailant's hand useless.

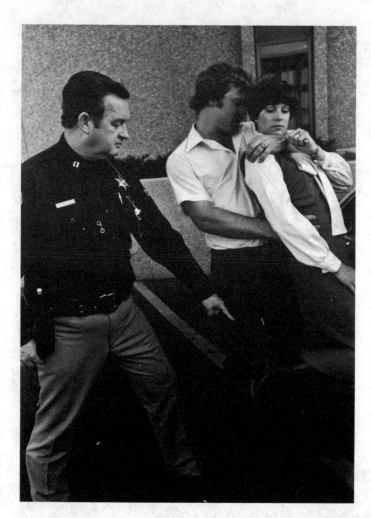

While jabbing with the key, the heel of the victim's boot or shoe can be driven against the attacker's kneecap (A).

Above: Striking backward with the key at the attacker's groin (A), can cause agonizing pain, even unconsciousness.

Right: Driving the point of the key into the attacker's throat (A) can lacerate his flesh and shock him with pain—perhaps even kill him. Trying to retain a grip on the attacker's clothing (B), the victim can kick him on the shin or instep with her heel or her whole foot (C), or drive her knee straight up into his testicles (D).

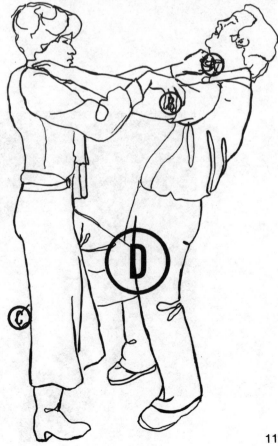

Notice how the driver stands next to the door and looks into the back seat of the car first. Most rapists hide in the front seat, however, with their heads down, holding the door handle inwards, ready to strike their intended victims with the side of the door as it is thrust open.

This shows what can happen next if you are not alert. The side of the door can knock you down with very little effort and with no chance of escape. Experienced police officers always stay behind the crease of the door on the driver's side when requesting driver identification. They know that a blow from only a small part of the door could knock them down or out onto the roadway.

This is what happened when the attacker suddenly threw open the front door. In this case, the driver will most likely sustain leg, back, or head injuries, rendering her helpless and defenseless.

With the driver on the ground and helpless, the rapist can now assault the victim or carry her to another location.

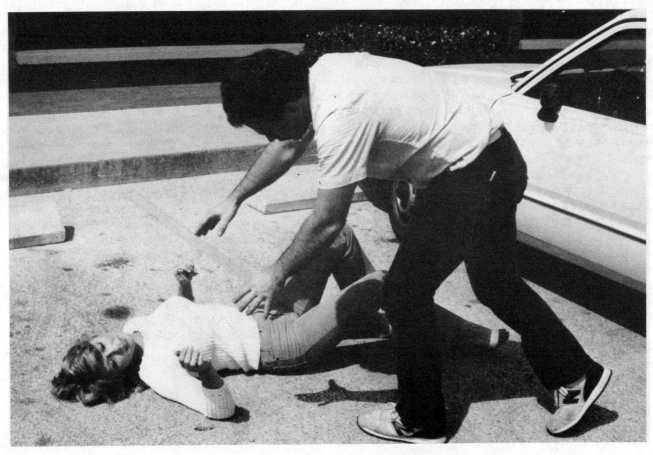

Safety Tips in Case of Car Failure

Whether you are the driver or the passenger of a car that breaks down on the road, where help is not close at hand, the following information will apply. Several tried and true methods are useful in this type of situation, whether you are driving alone or are accompanied by another female.

First, if you are stopped on a major highway, stay in the automobile and put on your emergency flashing light. Crack the window open slightly and tie a white handkerchief (or whatever is available) to the aerial. If there is no aerial, place the handkerchief outside the window and close it — this will hold the handkerchief in place. If a man other than a police officer stops to assist you, *do not* get out or even roll down your window. Whoever stops will be able to hear and understand what you are saying. Tell him to send a wrecker or alert the local police. Don't be fooled into opening the car door or leaving your vehicle.

One of the best anti-rape weapons you can carry in your car is a small (two-pound) fire extinguisher. Keep it right there on the seat beside you. If a potential rapist should ever try to force his way into your car, give him a good blast in the face with the extinguisher. If you feel you must leave your car for any reason, such as fixing a flat tire, be sure to carry your fire extinguisher with you. It is several times more effective than a can of mace; in fact, you would need a hundred cannisters of mace to equal the potential of one fire extinguisher. When fixing a flat tire, keep the extinguisher close at hand. If someone should approach your car, pick up the extinguisher at once. If an attack takes place, you can use the extinguisher in two ways. One is to spray your attacker in the face — this will temporarily blind him and cause him to choke. The other is to turn the extinguisher into an effective weapon with which to strike the attacker on the head or shoulder. Then be sure to seek safety at once. If nothing other than your car is available, get into it and lock the doors. This would be a good time to move your car onto the highway to attract attention. In fact, if you are caught without a fire extinguisher or some other defensive weapon, driving the car away is the

next best move you can make — even if there's a flat tire. Get the car moving somehow and blow the horn to attract attention. When all else fails to deter your attacker, slowly move the car to the center of the road. This may be taking somewhat of a risk, but with your emergency flashers on and a white handkerchief hanging outside your window, approaching motorists will be alerted to the fact that a problem lies ahead. At the very least, they should slow down. You can get help from either direction that way, and your attacker will be more than willing to leave you alone.

Many states are now giving out fluorescent safety signs in orange with the words "SEND HELP" printed on them. They can be seen at a distance of up to 200 feet. Because they are reflective, any oncoming traffic will be alerted to your danger and help should soon be on the way. Place the sign on the driver's side window and stay in your car until help arrives.

Should a man who comes to your aid seem hesitant to get involved or looks suspicious, you can always tell him you are a police officer's daughter or wife. Most men who entertain any thoughts about giving you a hard time will think twice about becoming involved with someone connected with law enforcement. If the suspect makes a comment about your license plate being out of state, for example, you can always explain that you are driving a friend's car. If that fails, stay as calm as possible and revert to other tactics discussed in this text.

Another tactic that has worked successfully for many women drivers is to tell the potential rapist that your boyfriend, husband, or father has left to get help and is expected back momentarily. This will put the intruder's mind on other things in a hurry. Whatever ploy is used, be sure you plan ahead for these contingencies. You must plant the seeds in your mind about the response you will give in any set of circumstances. Sadly, there is a very good chance that sometime in your life you will be faced with a situation where a plan of action will be essential to your well being. By thinking ahead, the proper responses are more likely to emerge when they are most needed.

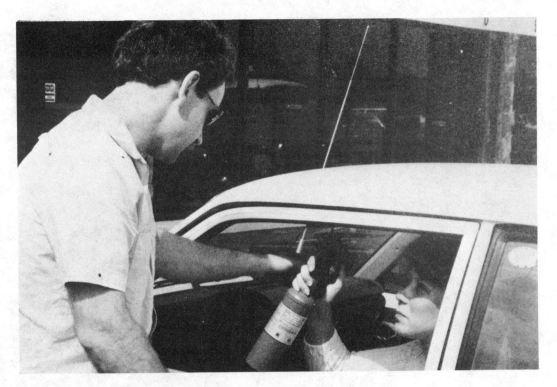

Should a rapist ever try to force his way into your car when it is stopped or in need of repair, and you have already lowered your window to talk to him, aim the fire extinguisher at his face and eyes as shown.

If your window is lowered all the way, the rapist may block your attempt to use the fire extinguisher, as in this case. Keep the window open only far enough to allow for the powerful spray to ward off the attacker.

If you must get out of your car for any reason, be sure to take some means of self-defense with you. Keep a fire extinguisher within reach at all times.

If attacked from behind, blast the rapist with the high-pressure extinguisher as shown. Other types of sprays can be used, but the results may not be as effective.

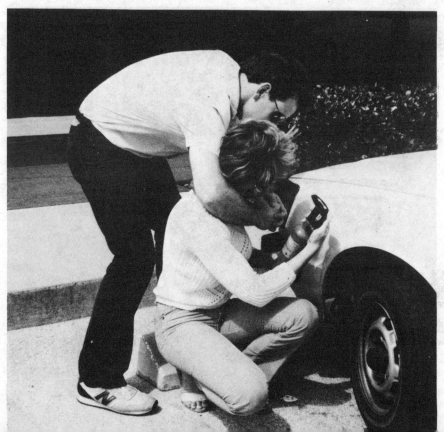

Notice how the rapist grabs for his eyes after being blasted by the fire extinguisher. The victim can now run for safety or give her attacker another shot.

If the victim cannot seek safety and her attacker has not given up, the steel cannister can be turned into an effective weapon, as shown here.

Here a woman driver is checking her car engine in a parking lot. Note the fire extinguisher close at hand and ready for use.

Using the front of her car as a shield, the intended victim lets go a blast of the fire extinguisher, repelling her attacker. Any high-pressure aerosol equipment can be used, but the type of extinguisher shown is by far the most effective.

127

The rapist has been forced to the ground and is holding his eyes in pain. He will also have difficulty breathing. Now is the time for the driver to seek safety.

When there is no alternative, it may be necessary to strike the rapist with the steel container, while he is still on the ground and vulnerable to attack.

CHAPTER 10

HOW TO USE A KEY TO DEFEND YOURSELF

A key, small and difficult to detect, can be an especially effective weapon against a rapist or any sort of unwanted attention. When an assailant's eyes are struck with the pointed end, it can cause serious injury, acute pain, and unconsciousness. As the attacker reels back, the victim can grasp his hair or clothing and stab at his face—or at any other body area—as often as necessary.

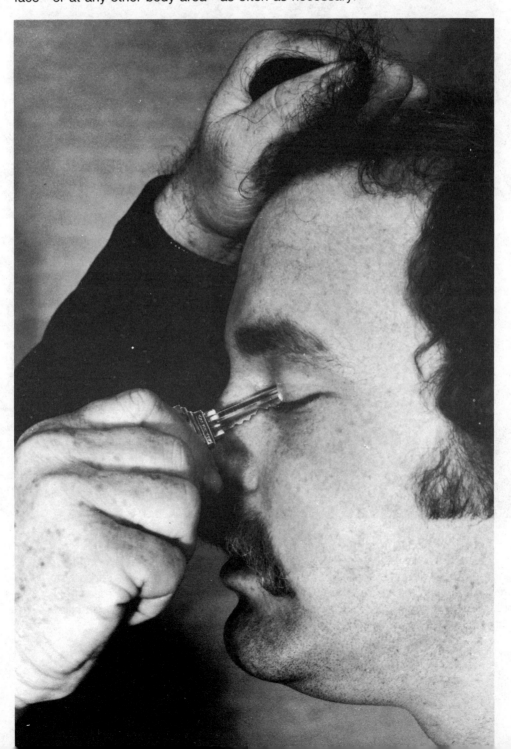

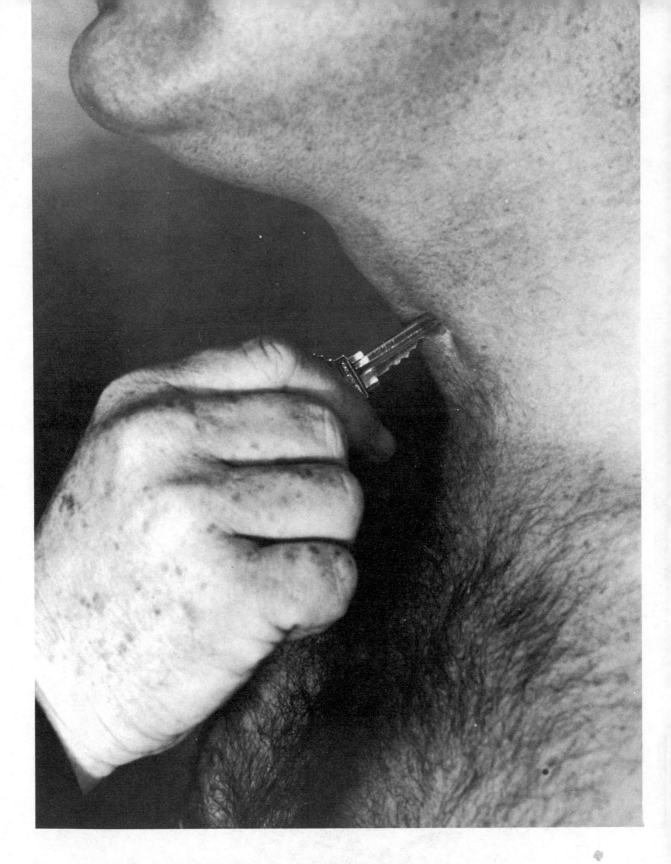

Driven into the tracheal tube (windpipe) a key can cause death. Stab wounds on either side of the windpipe near the carotid arteries, or in the soft nerve centers of the throat, may result in extreme pain, even loss of consciousness. Be extremely careful when practicing this defense; use only enough pressure to become familiar with how it is done.

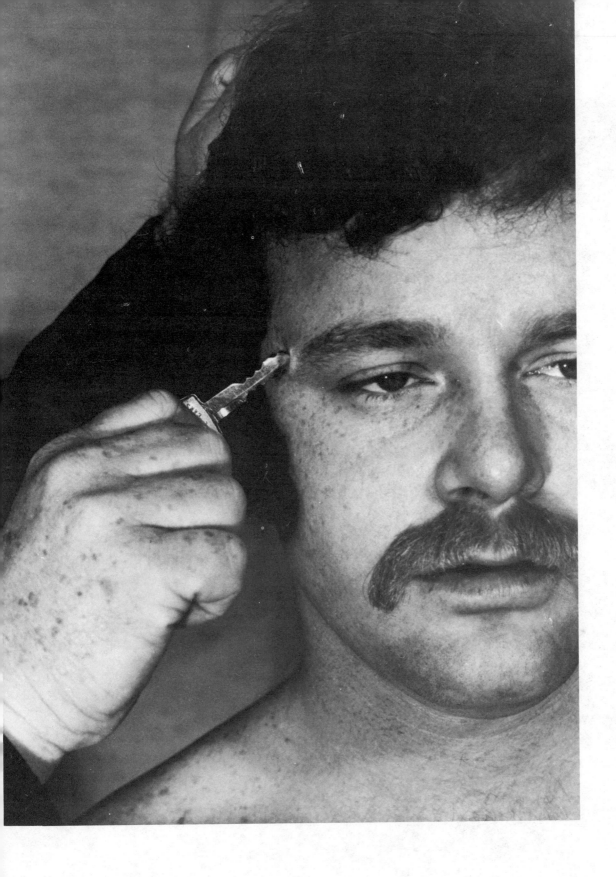

Using the point of the key, strike the rapist's temples or near the eyes. This almost always causes unconsciousness, and sometimes is fatal.

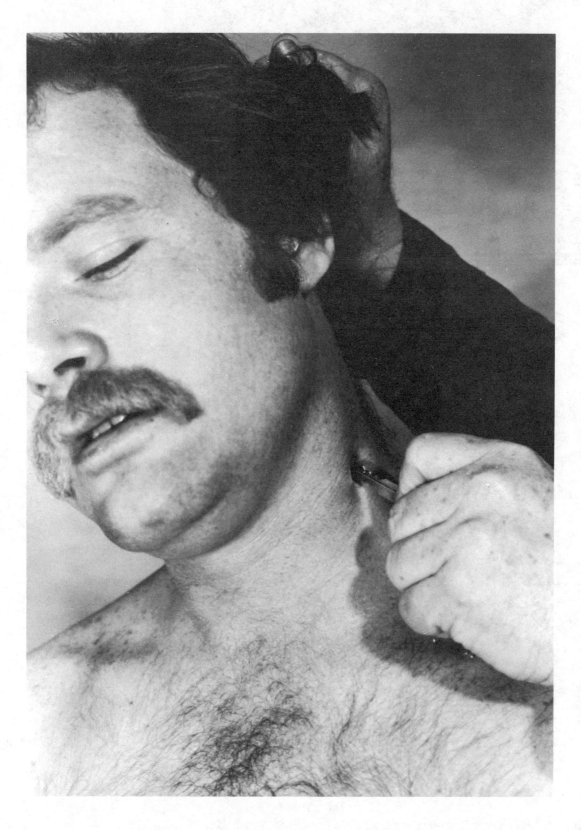

When pressed or struck into the side of the neck, a key can cause severe pain and injury. The victim will also be in a position to strike her attacker again.

Pressing, not striking, a key at the point shown below, a nerve center under the jaw, is quite effective at discouraging unwanted admirers.

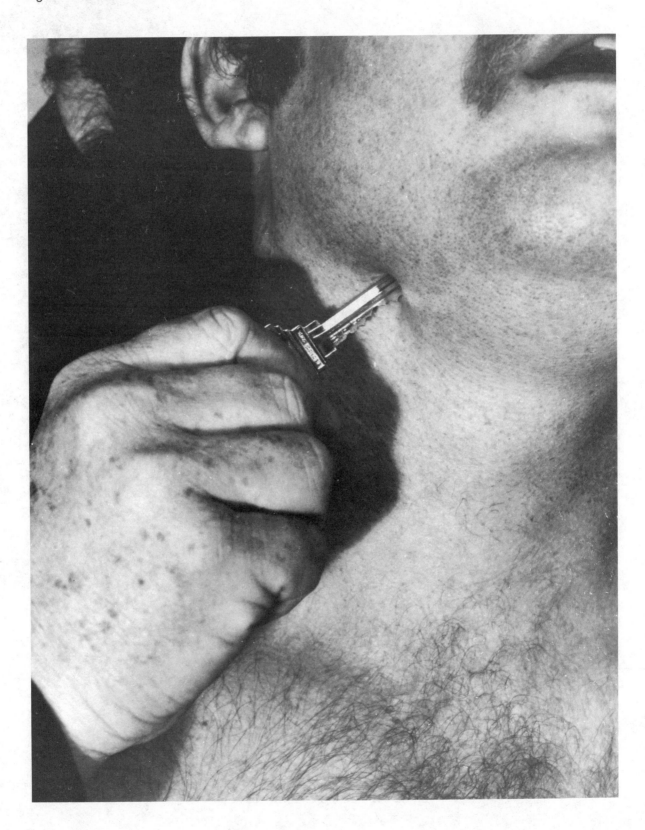

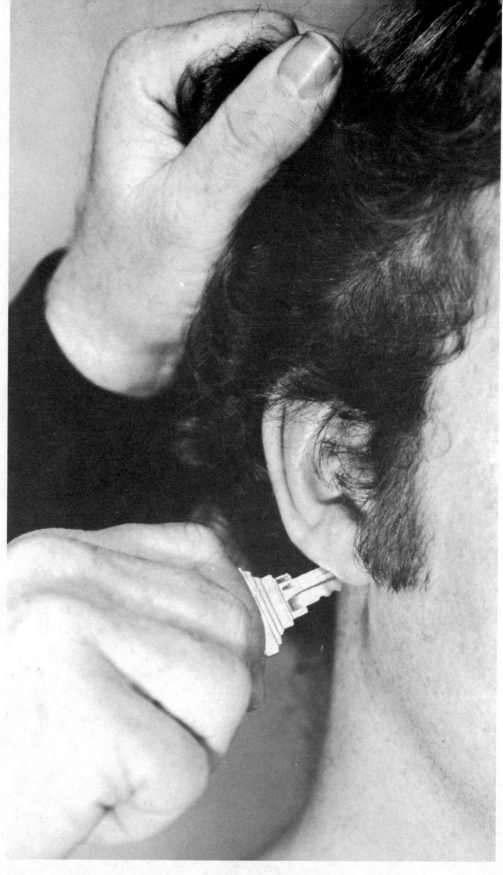

The nerve center behind the ear is very vulnerable. A stab in this area can cause great pain and permanent ear damage. The victim presses the key point in and then upward. This is an especially effective method of ousting an attacker from a chair or car seat.

The point of the key pressed into the hairline area at the nape of the neck can cause terrible pain; a jab wound sometimes results in death.

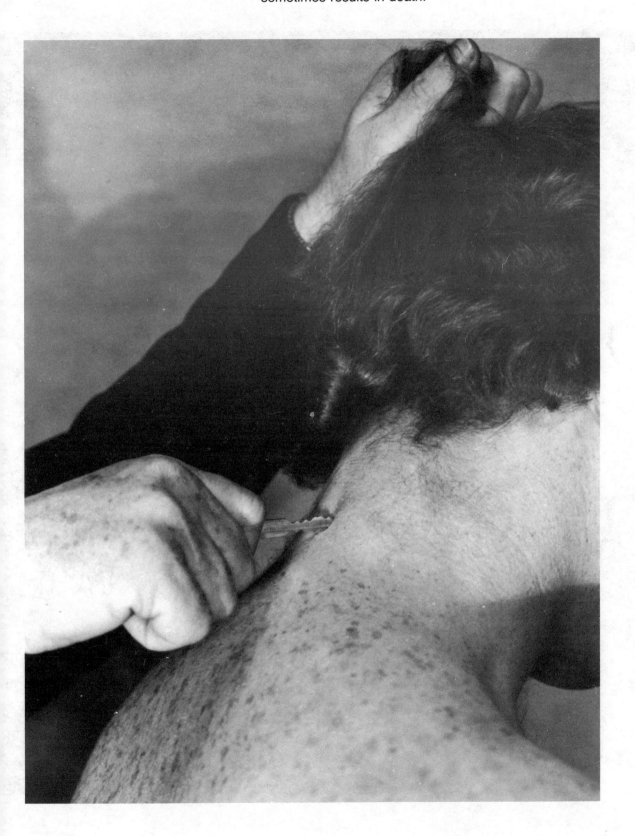

The point of the key pressed into the sensitive back of the hand can cause sufficient pain to bring an attacker to his knees. His grip can be broken when the victim's key punctures the skin of his hand, often breaking the small bones.

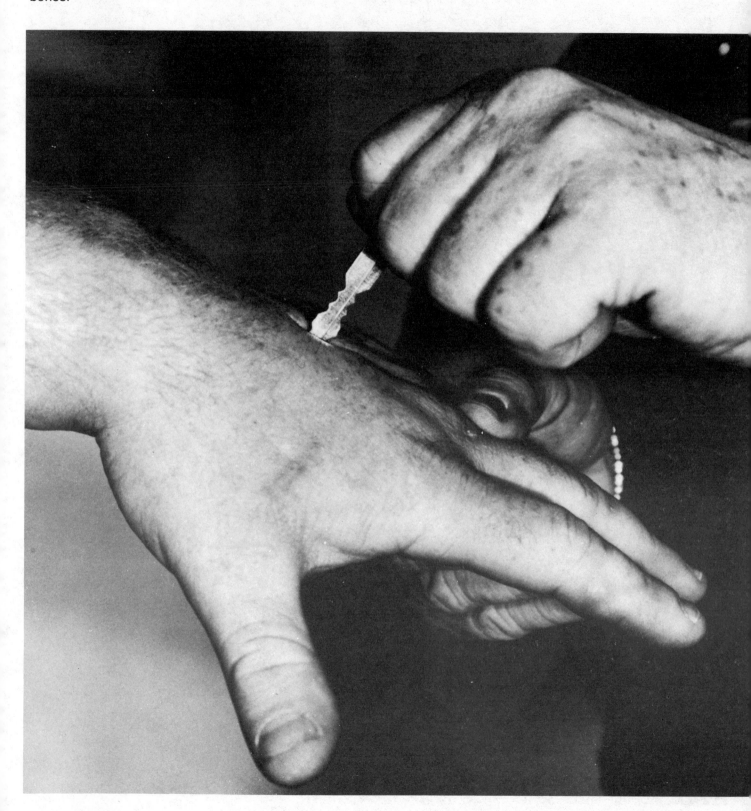

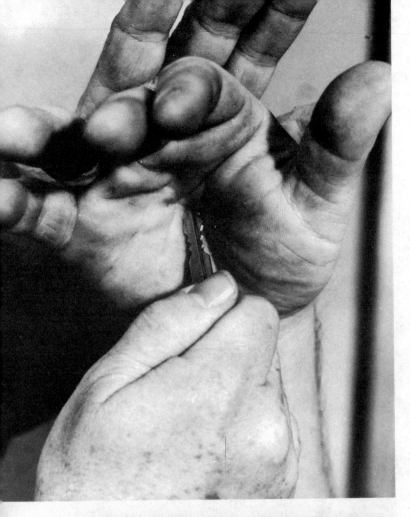

One way to discourage an attacker is to press a key upward into the palm of his hand while pushing down on the top of it.

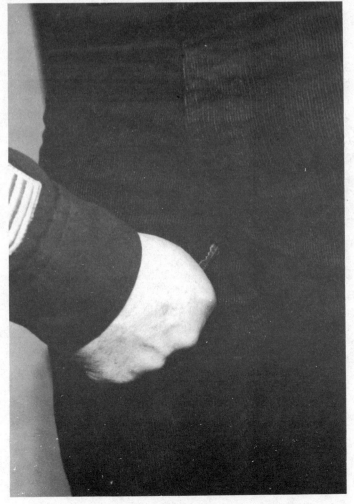

A jab of the key point into the rapist's groin is a blow serious enough to drop him, whether clothed or unclothed. More than one blow may be necessary in the case of heavy trousers.

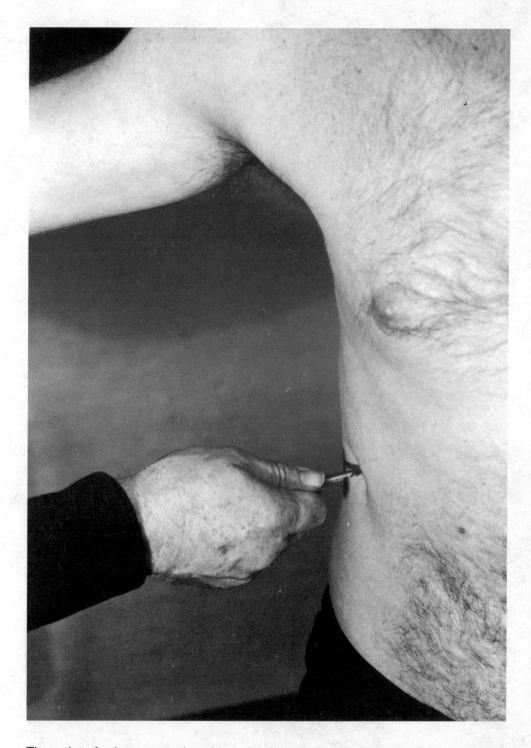

The point of a key pressed or driven into an assailant's rib cage can double him over, especially if the victim pulls his arm at the same time. A puncture could be fatal, or at least cause serious damage. This versatile defense is effective against attack in almost any locality or situation—a residence, a car, an alley, an elevator.

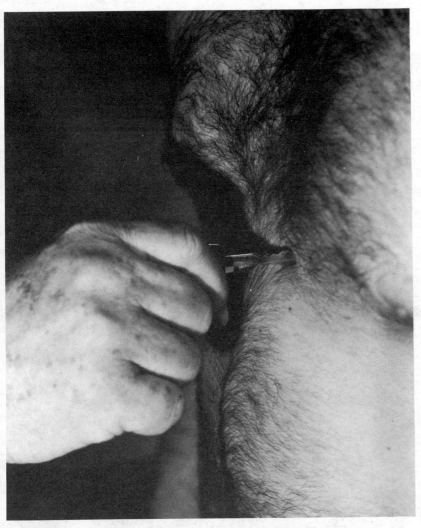

The point of the key pressed into the base of the sternum can freeze a rapist's movements, especially when lying down. If the victim is gripped closely in a standing position, she can press the key straight into her assailant's body.

If driven hard enough directly into the stomach, the point of the key can penetrate the flesh, causing debilitating pain and great damage to the underlying organs.

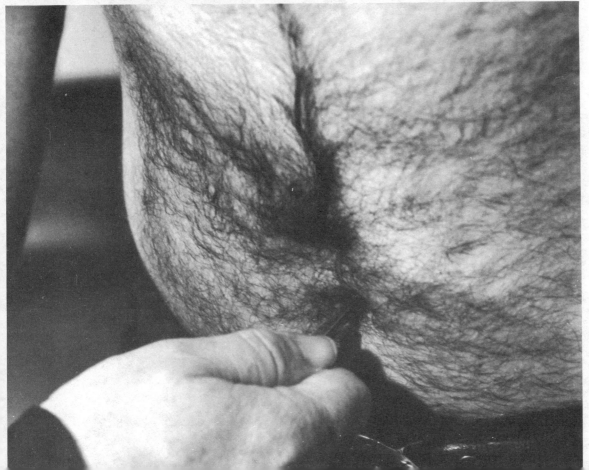

One of the most painful ways to use the key is to jab the point into the attacker's armpit, effective even through a shirt. By pulling his arm, the victim can stab quickly more than once, crippling the rapist with intense pain. A ball-point pen can substitute for the key.

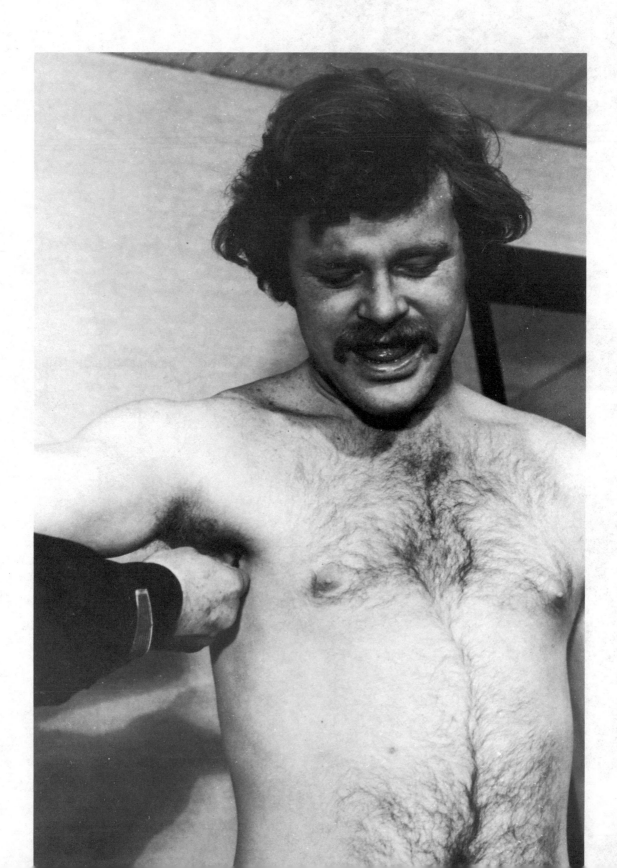

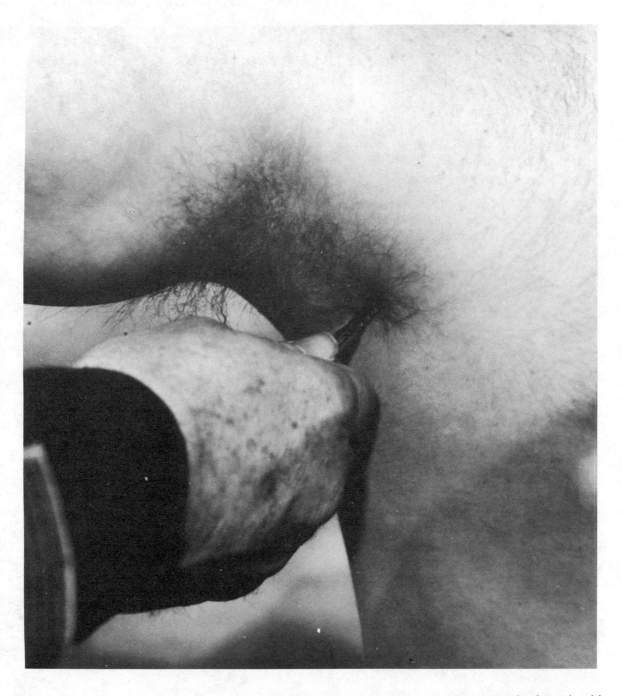

This close-up view shows exactly where the key should be jabbed for the most shattering pain—pain so severe, that the attacker will rise to his toes in agony. Be extremely careful when practicing the defense; use only enough pressure to understand where you should be jabbing.

The key can also be driving into the biceps—which will paralyze the arm and cause extreme pain. This method is particularly effective if the attacker is shirtless.

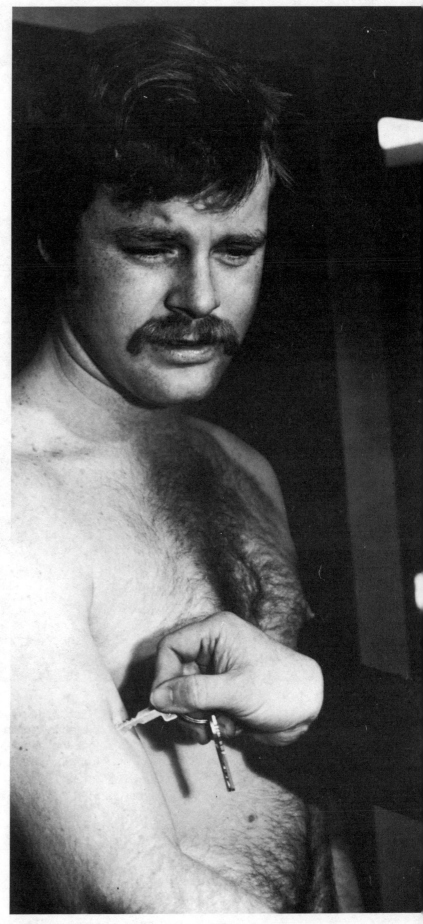

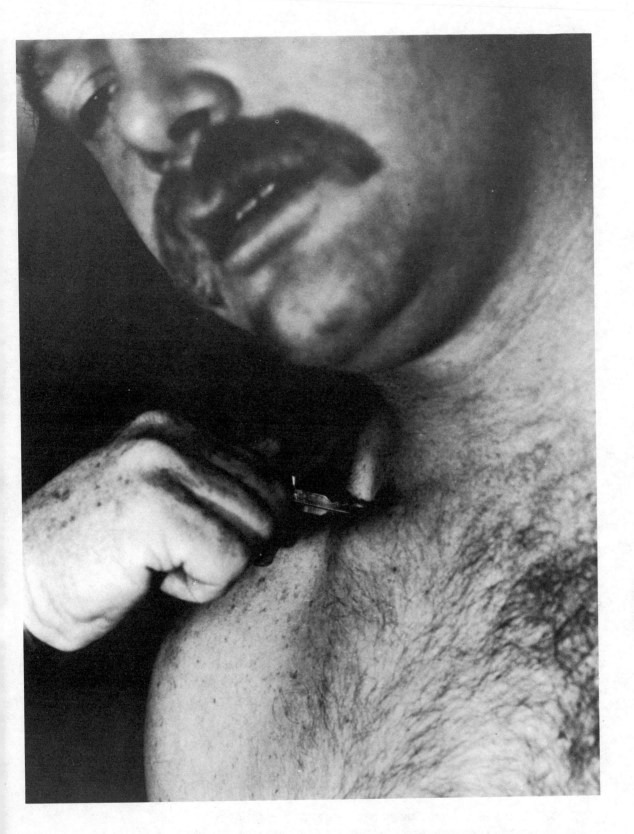

To bring an attacker immediately to his knees, drive the
key downward into his clavicle. He will sink with pain, and
the victim can then use any one of the follow-up techniques. This blow is effective even through a shirt.

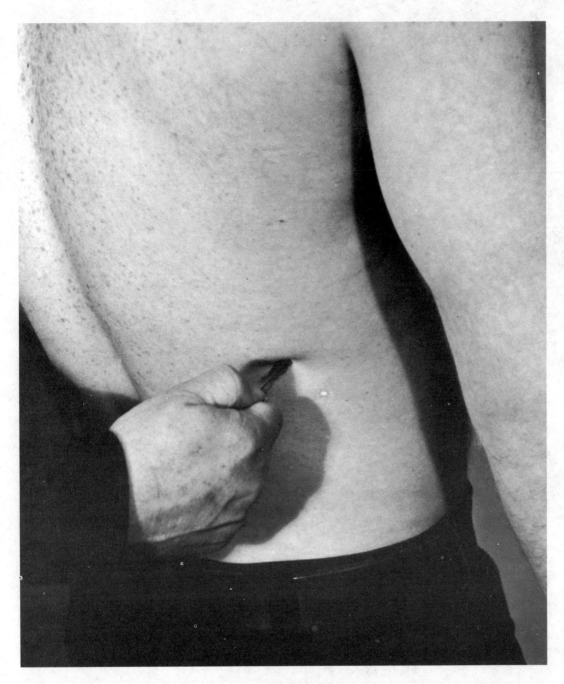

The key can also be driven into the rib cage from the back. With enough force, the key can penetrate the rib cavity and the kidneys, producing excruciating pain and almost instant unconsciousness.

The Magazine as a Defensive Weapon

A magazine, properly rolled, is even more deadly than a key. Any size magazine can be quickly rolled to form a pointed end. Grasping a magazine tightly approximately 2 to 3 inches from the point, it is possible to strike and break a 1x6-inch wooden board. In a defense teaching class, students stand behind metal folding chairs and make believe the back of the chair is an attacker's groin. Each student takes a couple of steps forward, then one step back, and hits the back of the chair while screaming "KIAI!" The chair will rebound about 6 to 10 feet. All students in the self-defense class must demonstrate this technique before passing the course. Even handicapped women and women up to the age of seventy-four have been able to execute the move successfully.

No attacker can withstand the point of a rolled-up magazine driven 3 to 4 inches into his groin. A blow of this sort will certainly disable him, maybe even knock him out. If the assailant blocks the attack with one or both hands, the victim can drop to the ground and drive up hard into the groin with either the magazine point or the blade of the hand. If gripped around the waist, the victim can drive the magazine into almost any body area—the attacker's temples, eyes, windpipe, forehead, stomach, kidneys.

Carrying a magazine should become a habit for a woman, and she ought to practice rolling it quickly and striking out with it in all directions. A magazine should be at hand in the front seat of an automobile and in every room of the home. Practiced with a friend in front of a mirror, the technique is quickly learned and proves amazingly effective. The key to successful use of any of these defenses is practice. The movements best suited to individual height, weight, strength, and mobility should be chosen and then practiced until they can be performed without thought. Combinations of moves can be worked out, such as using the knee or the snap kick in tandem with the key or magazine. A victim thus prepared can defeat almost any attacker.

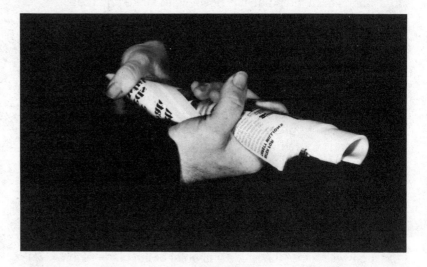

Note how the forward hand grasps the magazine, while the hand to the rear twists it so that a point protrudes. In the bottom photograph, the magazine is gripped tightly about 3 to 4 inches from the end, turning an ordinary article into a dangerous weapon. It will not crumple upon impact and can inflict a tremendous amount of damage. A magazine should be kept in a car and in every room so it can be quickly picked up when a stranger appears at the door.

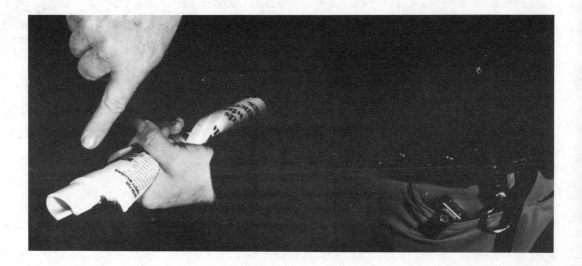

When first approached by a rapist, the victim firmly grips a rolled-up magazine and takes one step backward. The free hand goes out to stop the attacker's initial movement; the other hand is held close to the body in order to drive the magazine into his groin. The foot to the rear is in position for a snap kick or a knee to the groin. If the rapist is nearer, the magazine can be aimed at his head or throat.

147

Here a victim without much practice drives a magazine point at a 1x12-inch pine board, screaming "KIAI!" or "SUT!" for additional strength—and breaks the board in two. An attacker struck in this manner can be seriously or fatally injured—certainly rendered harmless.

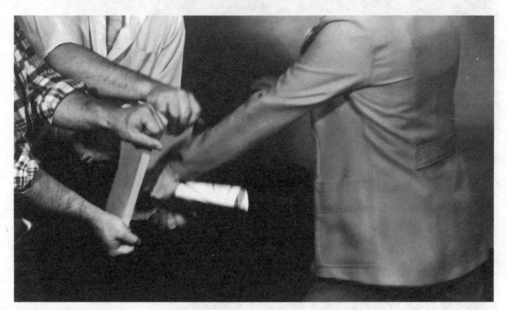

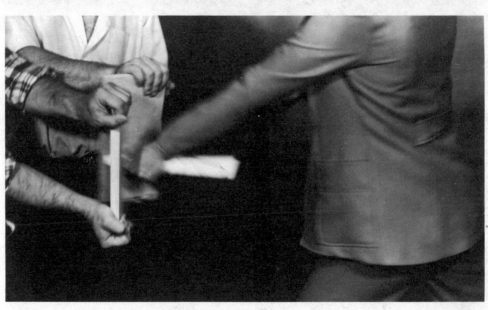

Left: The victim is in position with back foot in readiness; using an upward movement, the victim can drive the magazine into the throat of an attacker. Below: The victim repels an attacker who may be closer, driving the magazine point into his temples, eyes, face, or even rib cage, screaming "KIAI!" or "SUT!" for added power and confidence.

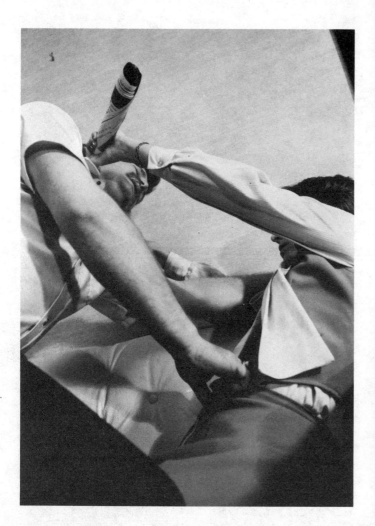

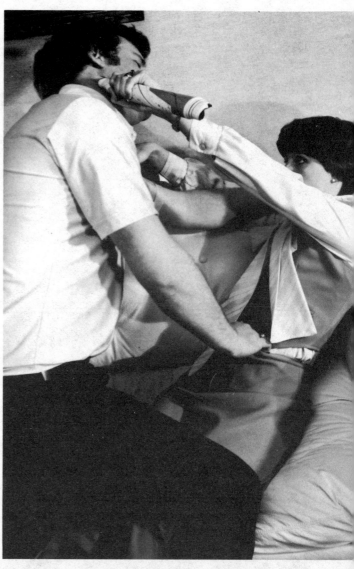

Once the attacker makes a definitive move—such as ripping away the victim's clothing—she can retaliate by stabbing a magazine point into the side of his neck below the ear, at the windpipe, or carotid artery, depending on her position.

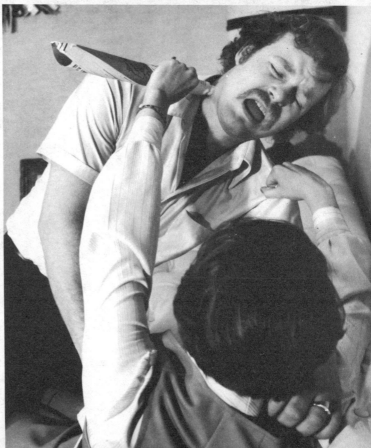

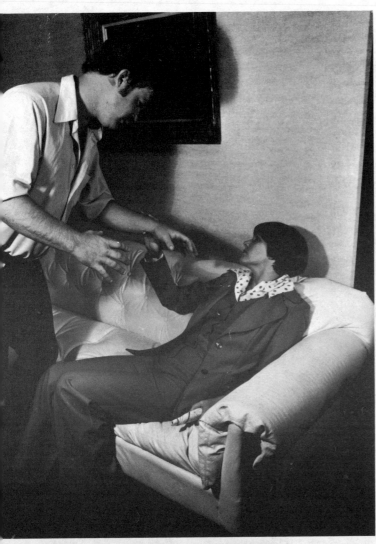

If the victim is approached by a rapist while on a couch or bed, she should allow him to place his hands on her—so she will know exactly where his hands are when she begins to defend herself. It is important to remain calm. Rape takes time—the victim must be stripped before penetration can take place—and a counterattack *can* be made.

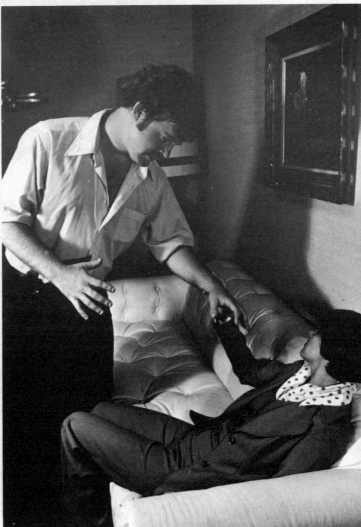

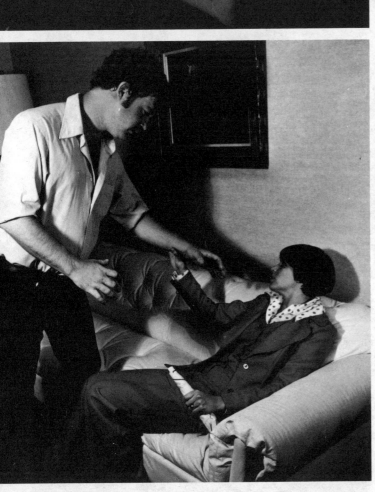

If the assailant is not wearing a shirt which can be grabbed, the victim should grab for his hair. Though he may be holding her by both arms, she can still drop to the ground and drive a magazine point straight up into his testicles. He will probably fall, writhing in pain, and she can then jab him in the rib cage, the temples, or the throat. Remember: both the magazine and the key convert quickly into deadly defensive weapons; practice with them.

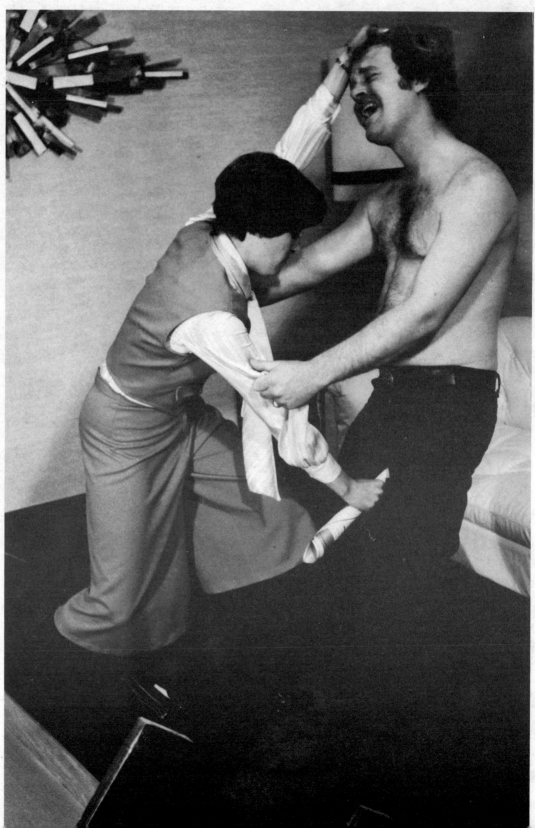

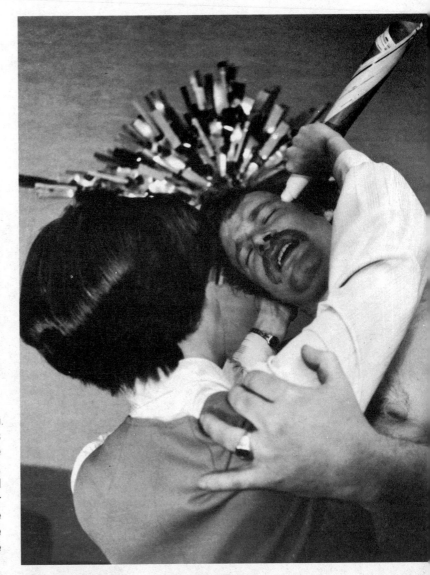

Right: Here the assailant is gripping the victim closely to him with both hands, protecting his groin. However, he can still be struck in the temple with the magazine point—or in the eye, the side of the neck, the mouth, the ear—and sent reeling in pain. Below: The victim jabs her attacker in the windpipe, at the same time grasping his hair. She can then knee him in the groin or strike him about the body with the magazine.

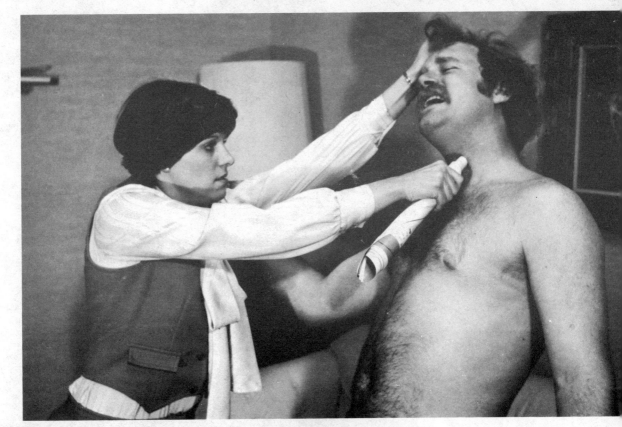

If the attacker hugs his victim to him, restricting her movements, she can stab him in the kidneys or the ribs; the pain will force him to release his victim immediately. Depending on her height, the victim can aim at the spinal cord or between the shoulders.

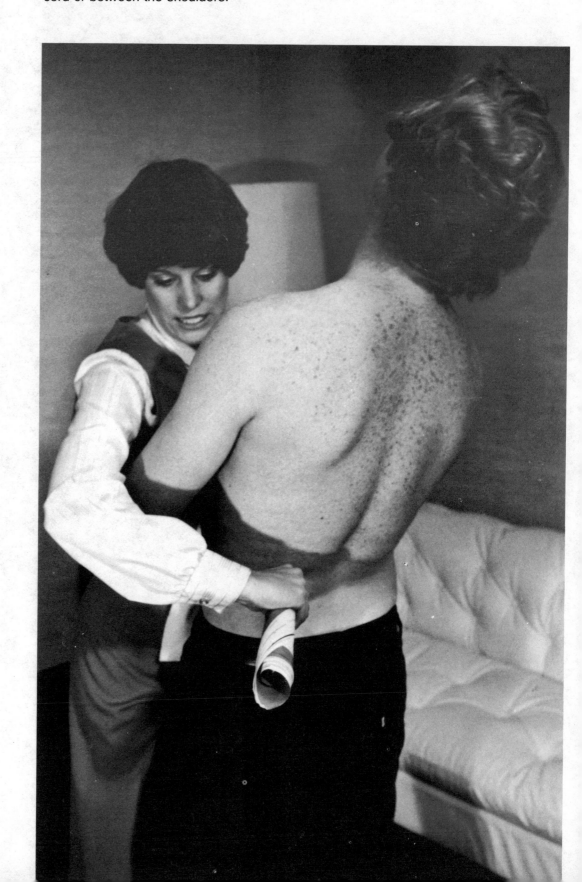

Defense Against Front Choke Using a Magazine

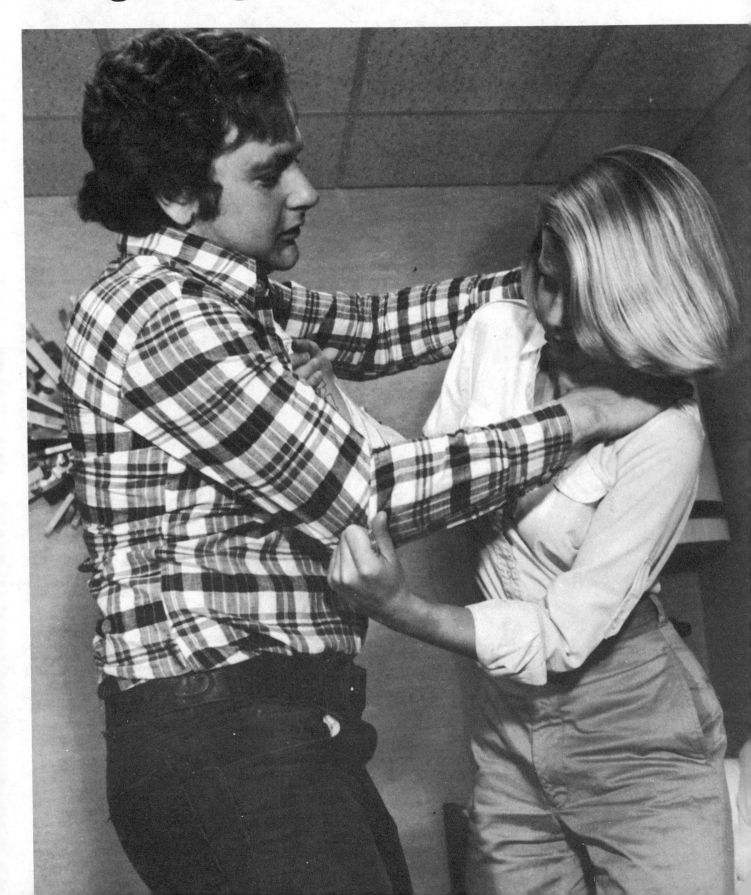

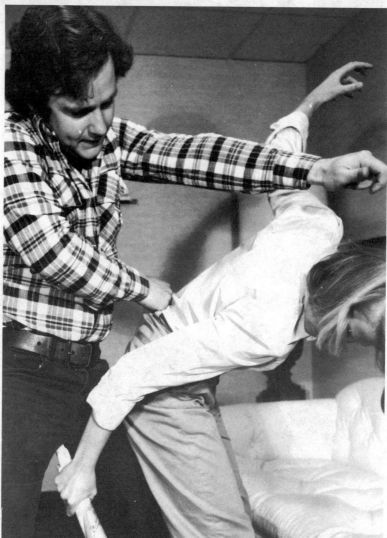

Above: The victim is attacked from the rear, grasped by the belt with head forced forward. Right: With one stiffened arm, she partially breaks her attacker's grip as she drives the magazine point backward into his groin.

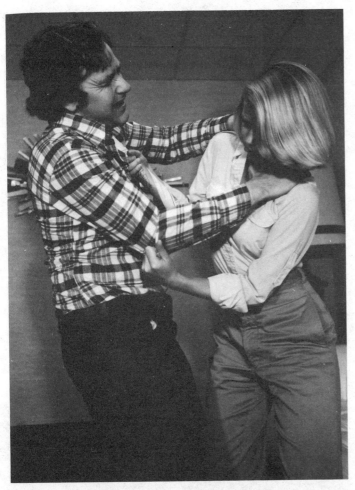

Left: A frontal choke is easy to break with a magazine. Grasping the attacker by one sleeve, the victim pushes her chin down on his hands to relieve the pressure of the choking grip. Then, with a quick thrust of the magazine point, she strikes him in the windpipe or tracheal tube. Below: A knee into the groin as she pulls him toward her should reduce him to complete helplessness. Below left: If forced backward or down, she can drop to her knees and jab the magazine forward into the testicles.

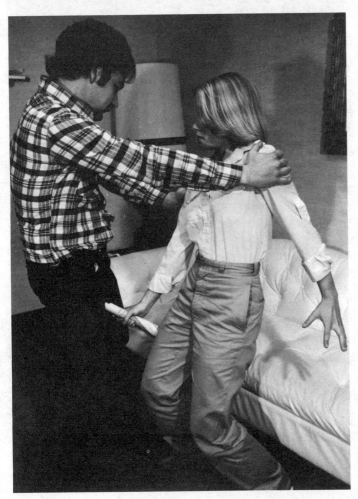

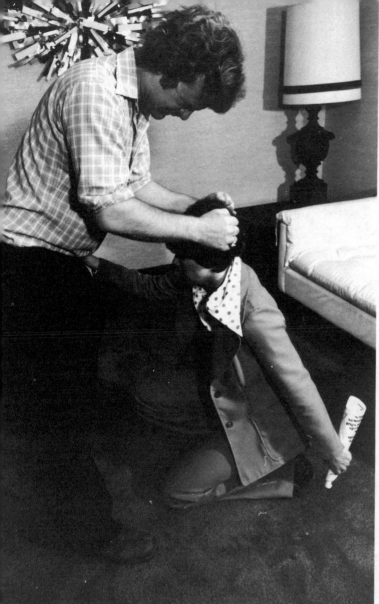

When grasped by the hair and pulled forward, the victim can drop suddenly to one knee and get a grip on the attacker's belt. Pulling herself forward by his belt, she can jab the magazine point repeatedly at his groin.

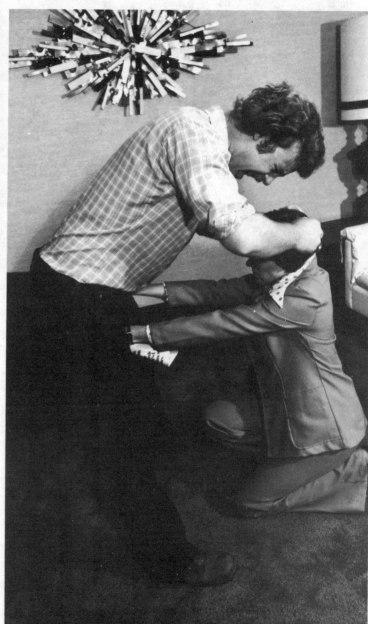

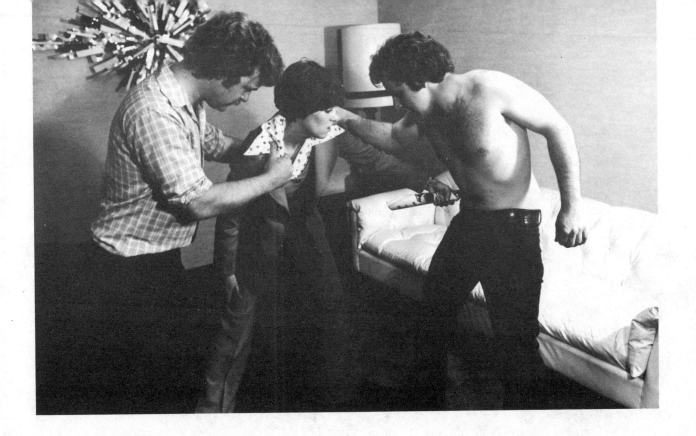

In the event of multiple attack, the shirtless assailant should be struck first—in the stomach with a sharp jab of the magazine. As he doubles up, the victim balances herself on his shoulders and brings her knee straight up at his groin, or snap-kicks him in the testicles or shin.

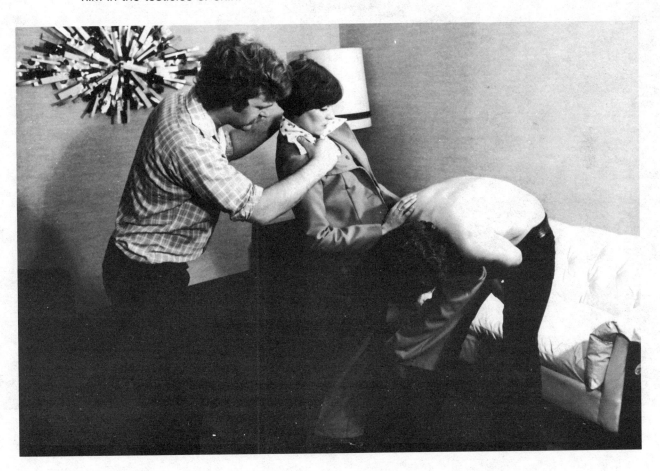

As the first assailant falls helpless, the victim drops and pivots, but now the second assailant has her by the neck. As previously instructed, she drops her chin to ease his choking grip, clutches his belt or shirt, and drives the magazine point upward from the ground, aiming for the testicles. Then she can stand up and butt her head into his face, or jab the magazine into his stomach, ribs, or face. With enough practice, the rolled-up magazine becomes an efficient deadly weapon.

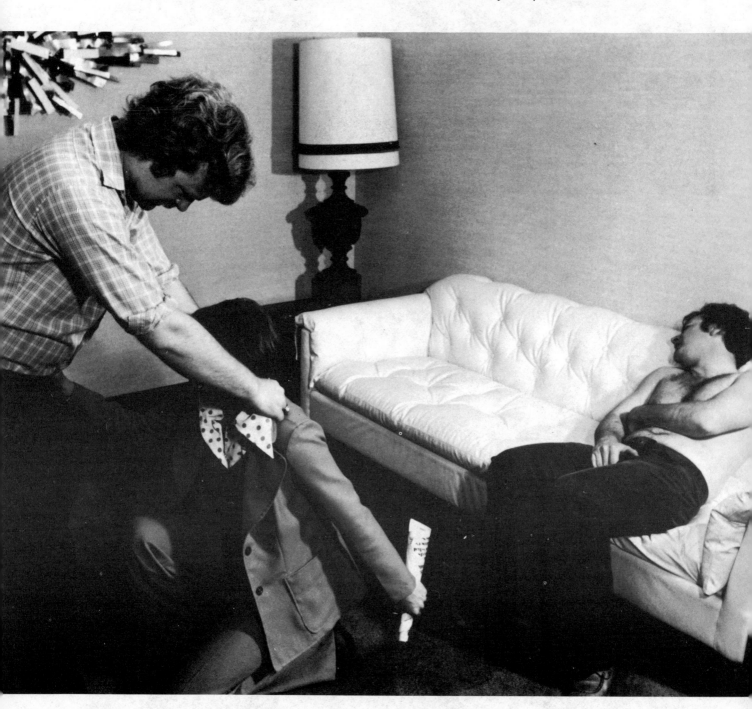

An ordinary book of matches is another potentially deadly weapon. Even non-smokers should carry a fresh package at all times. When folded diagonally from one corner to another, with one finger held on the folded edge, the sharp point can be used to jab an assailant in the temples, eyes, and throat. Pleading fear, the victim can ask her assailant to allow her a cigarette. Often, he will agree. Having pulled out her matches, she can then fold the book as if very nervous—during a nighttime attack this action is concealed—position her fingers, and strike out with all her strength. The matches can be folded in a split second, and if the victim screams "KIAI!" into the attacker's face as she lunges, he will instinctively move his head back, leaving himself vulnerable to attack. The victim may use any combination of moves—perhaps butting her head at his nose and following up with jabs from the matchbook, or jabbing first and then slicing at this throat with the blade of her hand. The more she screams, the more she will confuse her attacker, and thus increase her strength and advantage.

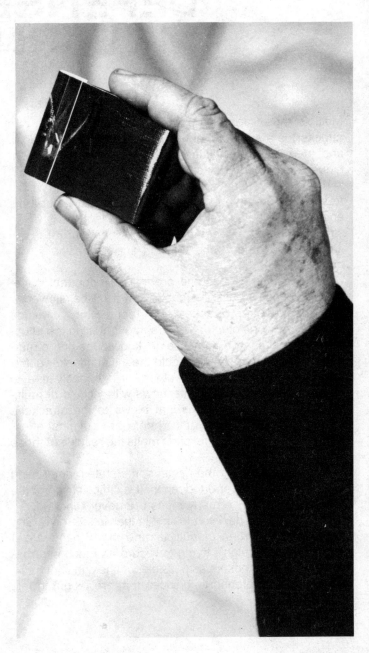

CHAPTER 11

DEFENSE AGAINST MULTIPLE RAPE

Multiple rape (rape of a single victim by more than one attacker) is a subject that has not been studied in depth, and there has been little publicity of the defense techniques developed against it. Multiple rape may begin with a blow to the victim's stomach. By the time the victim regains her breath and some of her composure, her arms and legs are being held down and she is already being stripped. In some cases the victim is beaten, but if she survives the ordeal, she will find she is, basically, unharmed.

The victim may become pregnant or contract a venereal disease, but in all probability she will be allowed to live because her attackers will fear facing homicide charges. Any one of the attackers, brought up in the future on a criminal charge, may use his knowledge of the murder to plea bargain. Also, should the initial attacker suffer severe injury or death, the others will probably flee to avoid involvement. From interviews with victims of multiple rape, the consensus is that blows to the attacker's back, along with the use of the heels, are the most effective. A determined struggle often melts the resolve of those waiting their turn.

Multiple rape is on the rise in some states, amounting to 52 percent of all reported rapes. It is difficult to compute hard statistics, since many rapes are never reported.

Ultimately, the decision to fight is the victim's own. She can endure the ordeal of multiple rape (in which the rate of survival is quite high), trying to record as much information about her attackers as possible, or she can fight back, using the self-defense techniques that are taught in this book.

Right: One assailant has gripped the victim's clothing, while the other is dragging her into the van. Note that the victim is clutching her keys in her hand. Many rapes occur in the increasingly popular vans, the small windows of which afford great privacy. When the music is turned up, the screams of the victim cannot be heard.

Below: The victim strikes the attacker who is holding her underneath the arms. Thrusting the point of the key through his flesh, she shatters the bones of his hands, and in his agonizing pain he releases his grip.

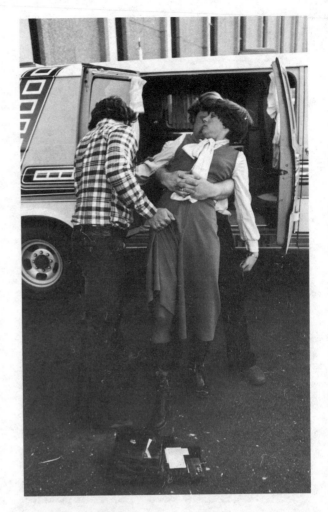

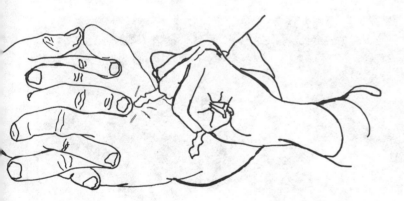

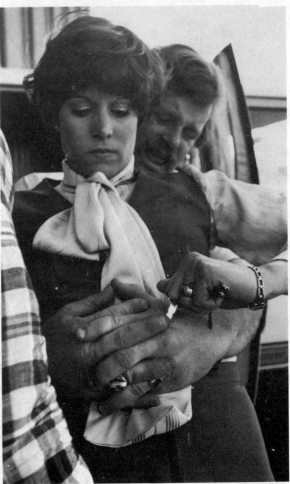

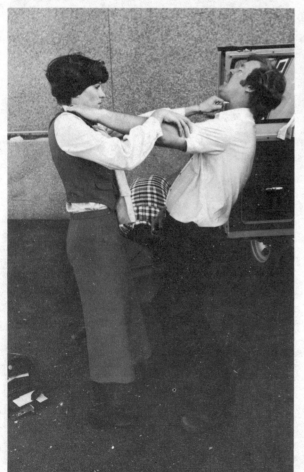

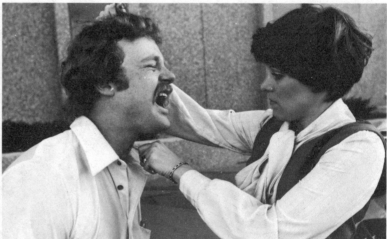

The victim turns to the second attacker, jabbing her key into his tracheal tube (A) and at the same time kneeing him in the groin (B). Pivoting, she grasps his sleeve and slashes at the side of his neck, or, holding him by the hair, she stabs him in the windpipe again.

Defense Against Two Rapists

Two rapists have converged on the victim, one caressing her stomach, the other holding her by the shoulder. They intend to push her to the ground, strip her, and assault her. Usually neither attacker knows the other's intentions, so defense against two rapists can sometimes be easier than against one, especially if the victim reacts aggressively.

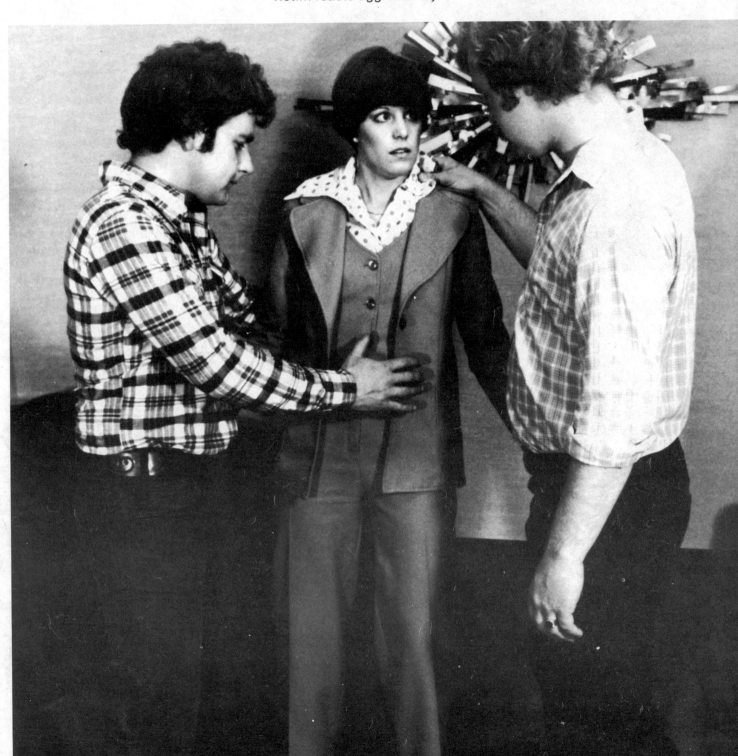

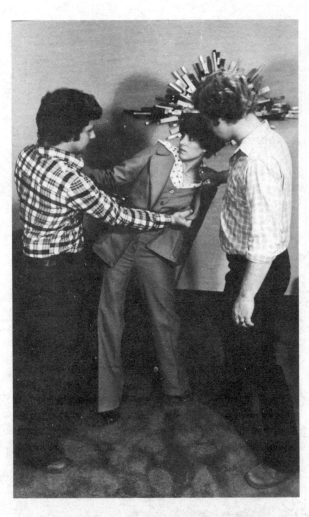

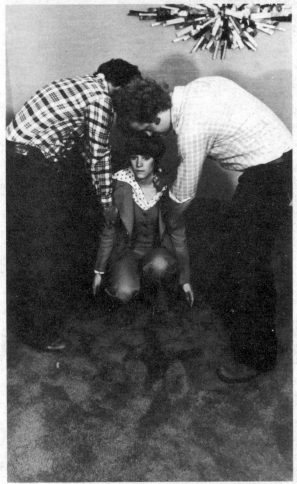

As one rapist pulls the victim by her shoulder, the other reaches to grip her jacket. She leans back and drops directly to her knees so that both rapists must bend to retrieve her. In the meantime, she prepares her hands (A and B) by maneuvering them into a position of vulnerability (C and D).

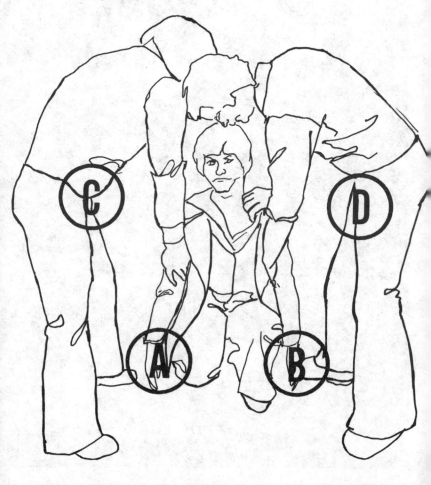

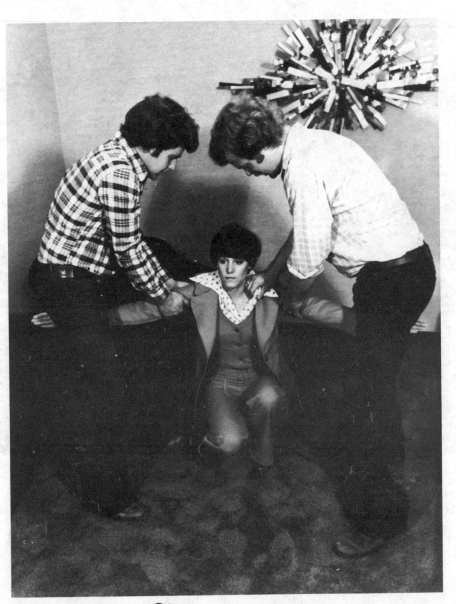

Though her shoulders are held by her attackers (A and B), the victim can extend her arms between their legs (C and D) and bring her forearm or wrist in a strong blow upward to crush their testicles—or she can pull her hands inward and squeeze the testicles.

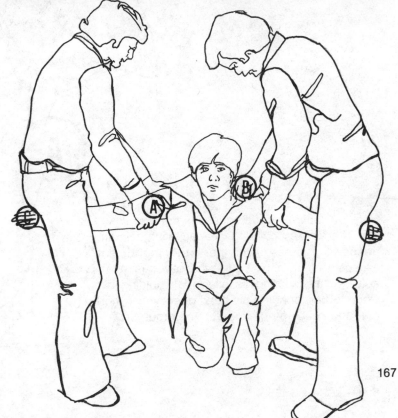

167

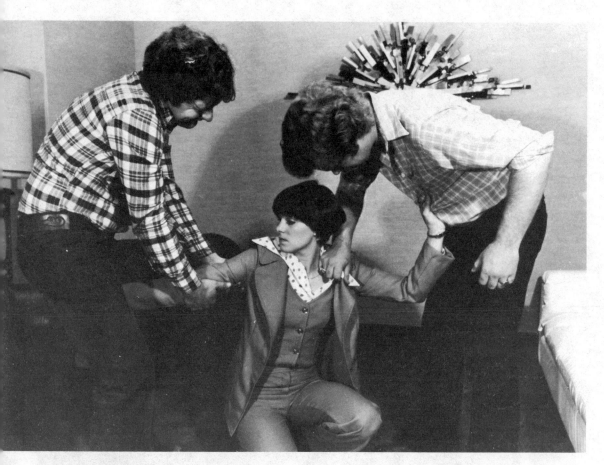

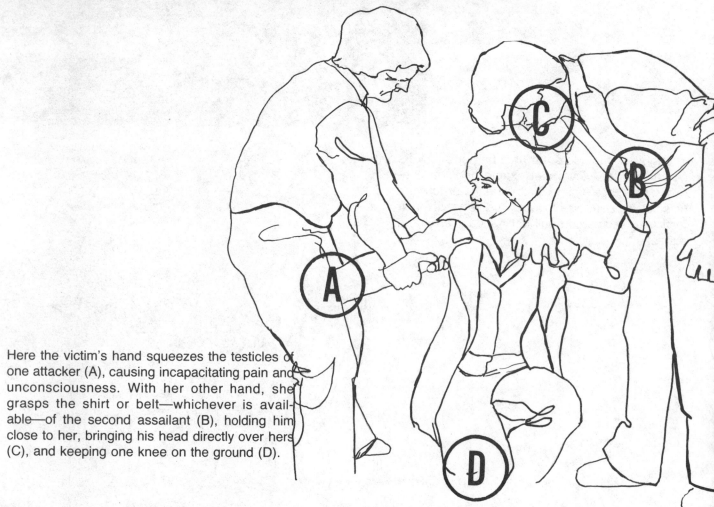

Here the victim's hand squeezes the testicles of one attacker (A), causing incapacitating pain and unconsciousness. With her other hand, she grasps the shirt or belt—whichever is available—of the second assailant (B), holding him close to her, bringing his head directly over hers (C), and keeping one knee on the ground (D).

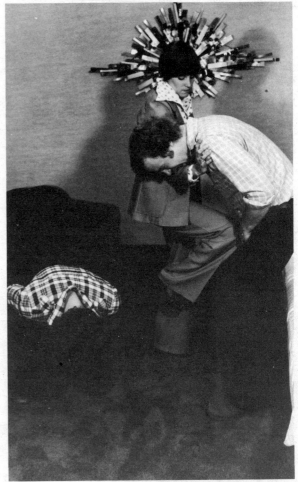

Springing to a standing position, the victim drives her knee into the second attacker's groin (A) while gripping him by his hair (B). The second attacker is now disabled.

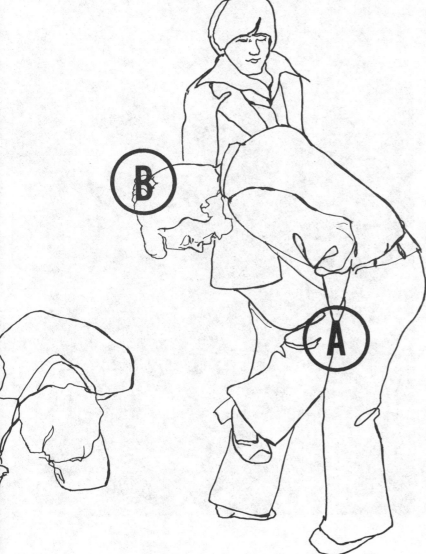

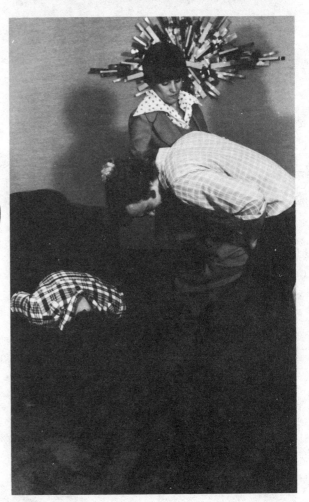

Defense Against Multiple Attack from Both Sides

When accosted from both sides by two or more rapists, the victim should drop instantly to the ground. Her attackers will attempt to pull her up, using her hair, arms, or clothing. As they bend to retrieve her, she should drive the blades of both hands into the groin area of both attackers. She can follow up with blows of her knuckles to the temples, her knee to the testicles, or her head to the face. It may be comforting to know that in the case of multiple rape, confusion often arises as one attacker hesitates, waiting for the other to act.

Immediately upon being attacked by two rapists, the victim drops to the ground on one knee. Grasping the belt or shirt of one of the attackers, she puts her hand between the legs of the other. They may attempt to pull their victim up or throw her back, but at this point each attacker is acting individually and the victim can take advantage of their confusion. If gripped by the hair and forced backward, the victim can clutch the belt of one while she punches or squeezes the testicles of the other. Having disabled one attacker, she pivots and, still gripping the belt of the other, she chops the blade of her hand into his groin, thus putting an end to the attack. In most cases of multiple rape, attackers rarely think ahead to prearranged signals, and a victim can use their lack of communication as another weapon in surprise self-defense.

CHAPTER 12

DEFENSE WHEN FORCED TO SUBMIT

When threatened with a gun or a knife, or with injury to another, such as a child, a woman may feel forced to submit to rape. But even during the course of such brutal trauma, she can attempt to defend herself or inflict serious injury on her attacker. Most rapists desire climax and humiliation of their victims, but there are also those who derive pleasure from sadistic punishment of their victims by using cigarettes, pliers, or whatever instrument of pain is handy. A women in danger of mutilation or fatal injury should defend herself even if it results in her attacker's death.

During rape, a woman should wrap her legs around the attacker's body, farther up his back than in the normal intercourse position, thus making penetration easier on her — and allowing her a chance to take action. One of the most vulnerable parts of the human anatomy is the spinal cord which encases a column of thirty-three vertebrae descending from the cervical to the base of the sacral and coccyx area (tailbone). Controlling the central nervous and the respiratory systems, the spinal cord is totally unprotected during intercourse. One of the strongest parts of the body is the heel, and as the rapist presses forward, the victim, with her legs drawn up around him, can drive her heels into his spinal cord within the lumbar area, perhaps severing it or breaking a vertebra and injuring a vital organ, such as the kidneys. Even if the heels miss the spinal cord and hit the tailbone area (the middle of the fanny), the victim can effectively injure the rapist and perhaps cause him agonizing pain. Naturally, the blow from the heels will depend on the physical size of the rapist and where the victim's heels will strike. Such a blow can result in death to an attacker, and if this prospect raises a moral question, any local authority can testify to victims who did not live through the rape.

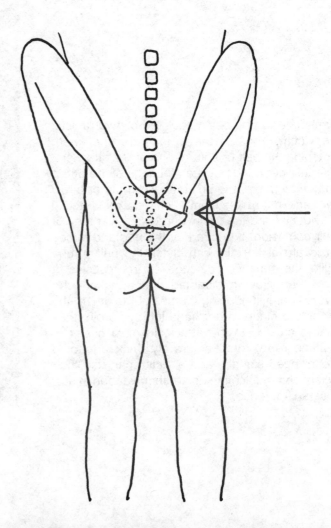

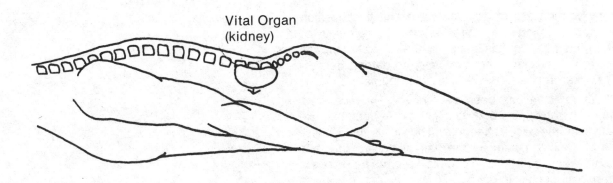

Vital Organ
(kidney)

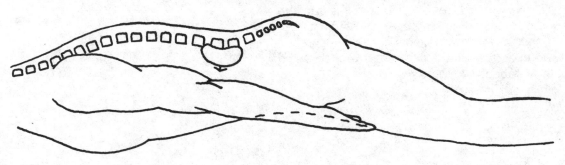

Location of Kidney
with Body in Raised Position

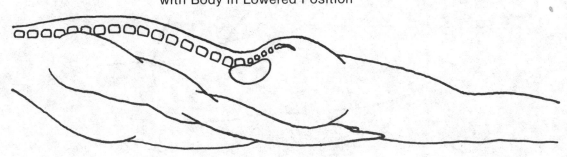

Location of Kidney
with Body in Lowered Position

173

Many women are raped face-down and this position makes identification of the attacker difficult, especially at night. In this position, it is easier for the rapist to strip his victim and more difficult for the victim to defend herself. The attacker may also desire anal intercourse.

When a victim has been penetrated in a face-down position, the attacker's body is aligned with hers, his face directly over the back of her head. The victim should raise her hand and grip him by the hair or collar, and then smash the back of her head into his nose. As he recoils in pain, he will penetrate deeper. At that instant, the victim snaps her leg and body straight, preventing the attacker from withdrawing and inflicting excruciating pain on him. The victim then rolls over to strike at his throat or groin area. If she is able, the victim should leave the injured rapist and seek safety and the police. This defense, most damaging to a rapist, is also somewhat painful to a victim, but it is the only choice over rape and the mental and physical wounds that accompany it.

This defense technique was developed from a story related to the author. A woman was arguing with her husband and did not want to have sexual intercourse from the rear; the man succeeded in his penetration against her will. In her anger, the woman snapped into a straightened position, and used the head technique. The man could hardly walk for about two weeks!

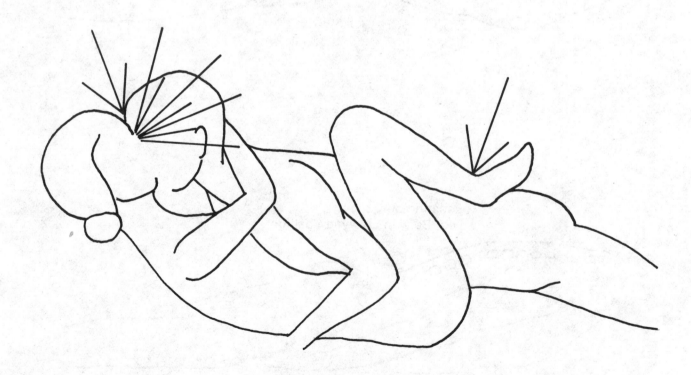

CHAPTER 13

WHAT TO DO WHEN A DEADLY WEAPON IS USED

When confronted with a deadly weapon such as a gun or a knife, it is best to submit and wait for an opportunity to take defensive action, even though this may mean experiencing involuntary intercourse. Rape takes time; there will come a moment when the attacker will put down his weapon and the victim can defend herself, even if her hands are tied.

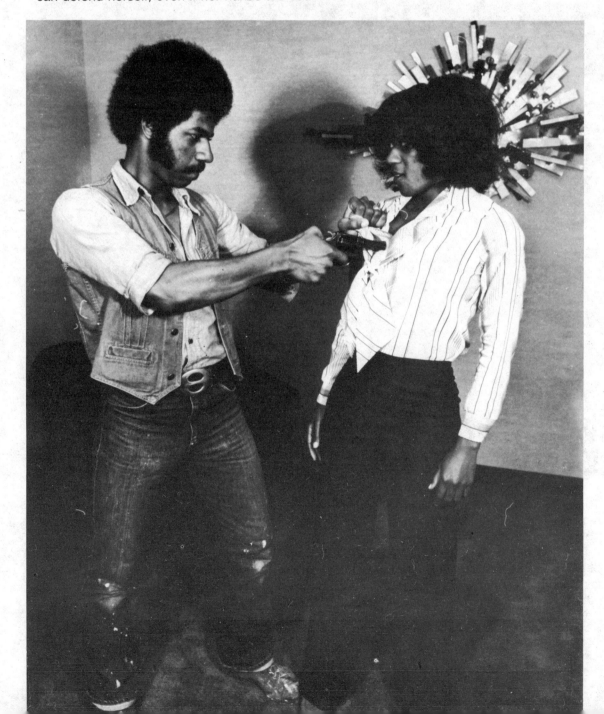

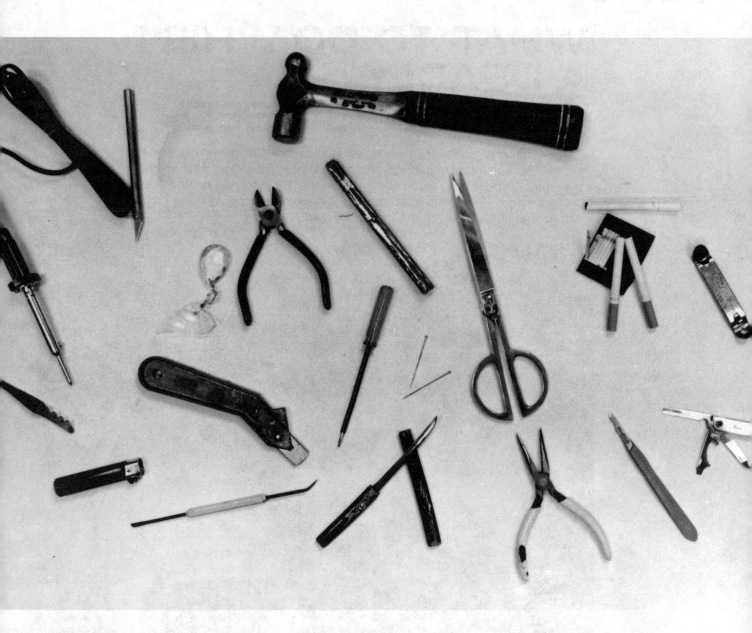

Weapons Used by the Deviate Rapist

These common objects—scissors, pliers, blades, tweezers, matches, cigarettes, cigars, soldering and heating irons, sharpened can openers, a piece of glass, a lighter—have all been used by rapists on their victims before or during sexual attack. Permanent mutilations and lasting mental trauma have often resulted. The knowledge that such weapons—along with guns and knives—have actually been employed to stimulate and subdue women is reason enough to study the art of self-defense. An attacker who uses any of these weapons is a sadistic deviate, and a victim need have no compunction about using as brutal a defensive technique as possible against him.

CHAPTER 14

HOW TO HANDLE A SEXUAL GROPER

Most women have, at one time or another, encountered unwanted sexual attention. Merely saying no may not be enough, but it is important to repel the aggressive fondler before the situation gets out of hand.

Above: The victim grasps the hand on her breast—as though enjoying the sexual attention—and pulls downward on the fingers, causing the muscles and bones of the hand to protrude. Below: At the same time, she frees her other hand, clenching the knuckles into the V formation. Locating the target area, the victim draws her knuckles back 8 to 10 inches and then drives them into the back of his hand, possibly fracturing some bones, and certainly dissolving his embrace.

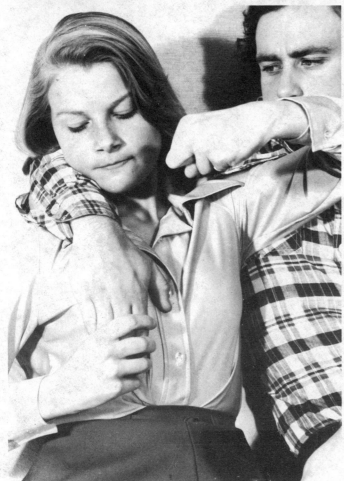

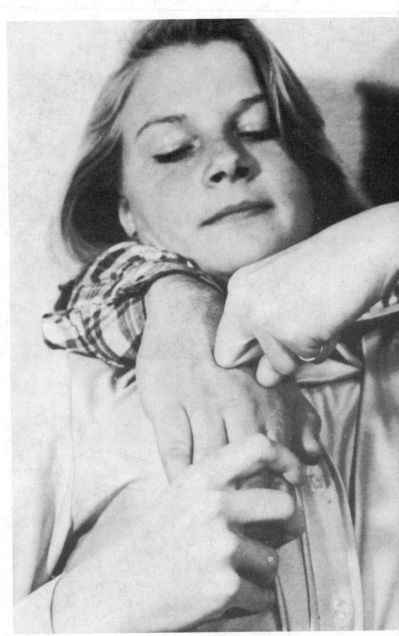

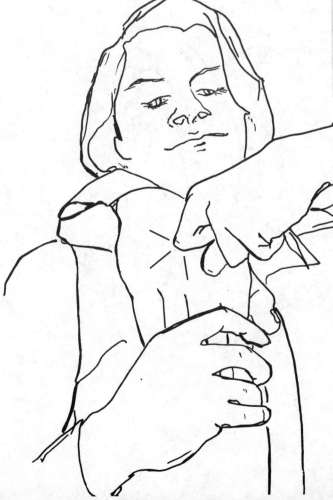

The victim pulls the man's hand taut, exposing and locating the target area, taking care to avoid hitting herself.

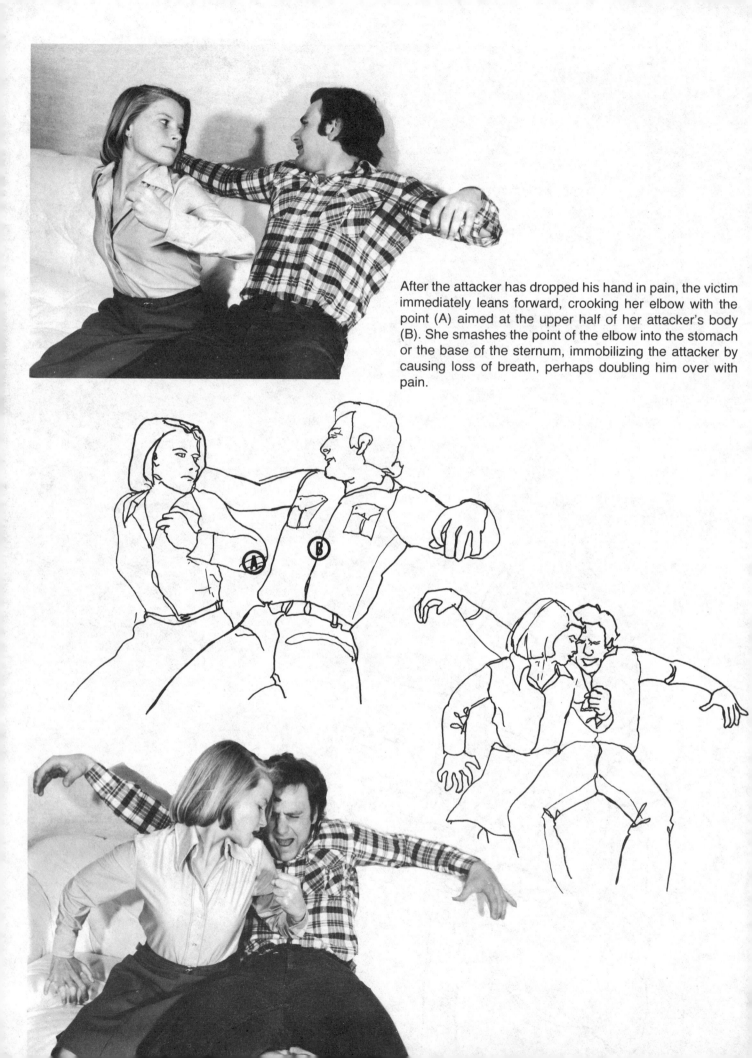

After the attacker has dropped his hand in pain, the victim immediately leans forward, crooking her elbow with the point (A) aimed at the upper half of her attacker's body (B). She smashes the point of the elbow into the stomach or the base of the sternum, immobilizing the attacker by causing loss of breath, perhaps doubling him over with pain.

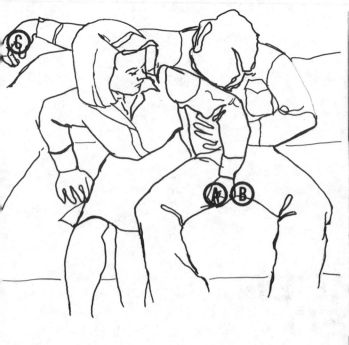

If her attacker persists after being struck in the stomach, the victim can bunch her fist (A)—still in the knuckled V formation—backward into the testicles area (B). If that blow is ineffectual, she can bring her hand forward and drive her elbow back into his throat, perhaps crushing the tracheal tube. Potentially lethal, this blow should only be used in extreme cases, when the victim feels that rape is imminent. Normally, the knuckles to the hand and the elbow to the stomach are sufficient to deter the sexual fondler.

CHAPTER 15

POINTS TO REMEMBER IF ATTACKED

In the event of attack, the victim should always try to turn her body so that her shoulder faces the attacker's chest and outstretched arms. This position makes it easier for her to grip him by the shirt and more difficult for him to grasp her neck or belt or to get his arms around her. This stance also puts the victim into position to snap-kick into her attacker's leg or groin. She can also pivot in his direction to drive her foot into the side of his kneecap or smash her knuckles against his temples. When she pivots, the victim forces her attacker forward, thus baring his throat to the blade of her hand. Or, she can pivot on her front foot and kick with her other foot behind the kneecap of *his* leading leg, bringing him to the ground with a crash. Another pivot and she can knee him in the face, throat, or temples.

When attacked frontally, a sudden scream or series of screams into the attacker's face will always disorient him, forcing him to recoil involuntarily. As she screams, the victim can drop to the ground, chopping or kneeing him in the testicles as described. Any movement, or series of movements, can then be used—a butt at the face or stomach and a knee in the groin, a butt at the face and a side kick at the kneecap. The scream can precede or accompany any number of defensive moves—the V fist into his throat; stiffened fingers into his eyes; elbow into his face, throat, or temples. His hair can be grasped and his head pulled down for a knee in the face.

If completely off guard when attacked, the victim should try to remember to drop to the ground, gaining time to place her feet for defense. As the attacker moves in, she can get one foot behind him and go for his forward knee-cap with her other foot. This will send him staggering, freeing the victim to regain her control or to escape. Lacking keys, a magazine, a matchbook, or a pen, a victim with her wits about her can use her body for effective defense. The initial assault is shocking, but the victim must remember that the rapist really cannot proceed until she is forced against a wall or to the ground. And in that interim, she *can* defend herself.

The snap-kick is an integral component of defense technique against rape and should be learned with all its variations. Balance on one leg, bend the other leg slightly, then draw the foot up along the side of the straight leg. As you snap-kick forward or back, scream "KIAI!" for additional strength and power and to startle your attacker. For the first few weeks, ten minutes of daily practice is urged until the technique becomes automatic. As a plus, the exercise helps to condition the body and tone the muscles.

Left: In snap-kicks to the side, you drive your foot into the attacker's kneecap or your heel into his groin. The movement should be practiced alone to achieve balance and then later with a partner. A straight-kick allows an attacker to catch the victim by the leg, but a snap-kick is quick darting and keeps the victim on the offensive.

When practicing the back-kick, a pillow stuffed with rags and hung from a doorway makes an effective target. Frequent daily practice will improve aim and bolster confidence, as well as sharpen judgment of how much power is needed.

In the starting position, the body is rigid with one foot slightly raised. Keeping back and arms straight, lift the leg to approximately the height of the other knee, which is slightly bent for balance. From this position you can snap-kick to the front, side, or rear.

Right: In the multiple attack, the victim grasps the shirt of the frontal attacker. Hanging on for leverage, the victim snap-kicks back at the rear attacker's knee.

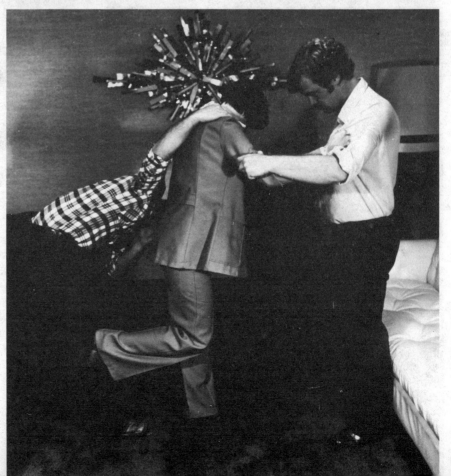

184

Left: As the victim snap-kicks, she draws back her knuckled V-fist for a follow-through blow at the attacker's windpipe.

Below: The effective use of the knee. Extend the hands approximately the level of the attacker's groin. Step back from the presumed attack keeping both feet flat on the ground, shoulders and back straight and eyes focused on the target. Powerfully thrust the knee forward from this back position and scream "KIAI!" as you drive at the groin area ,(as shown in top photo on page 184)

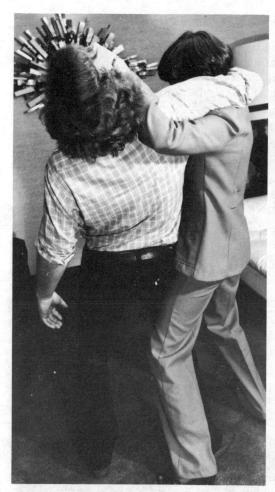

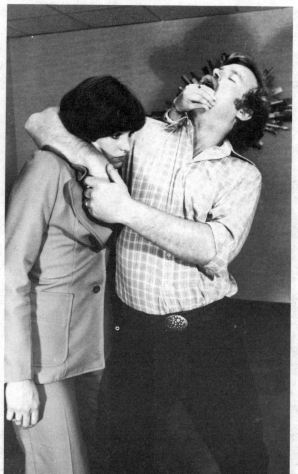

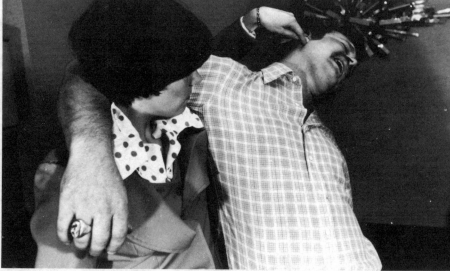

When attacked from the side, the victim maneuvers one leg behind her attacker's kneecap and raises the hand on that side over his shoulder to the area beneath his chin. By pushing forward with the knee and backward with the hand, the victim can knock the attacker off balance and expose his abdomen for a strike at his testicles with her fist or the blade of her hand. Since she has also thrown her attacker's head back, his throat is a wide-open target, and she can slice at his windpipe with the blade of her hand or chop him in the trachea with the knuckled V. To discourage unwanted attention without causing injury, the victim can merely poke her finger into the soft area just under the earlobe and drive her fingernail into the flesh and up. The pain that results will destory the attacker's amorous mood.

In another defense to a side attack, the victim grasps the attacker's belt—with fingers down—while distracting him with a sensuous move. She puts her hand on his shoulder (right), steps forward, and pulls him toward her. Below: Raising her arm across his throat, she pushes forward on the belt and back against the windpipe forcing him to walk backward. If the victim genuinely fears rape, she can strike the attacker in the throat, holding his shirt as he falls, and then drive her knee into his groin (below right). Or she can grasp and twist his shirt collar, which will probably choke him. If the attacker falls to the ground, the victim can kick him in the groin or stomp his throat. Caution is urged when practicing these moves to avoid injury to a partner.

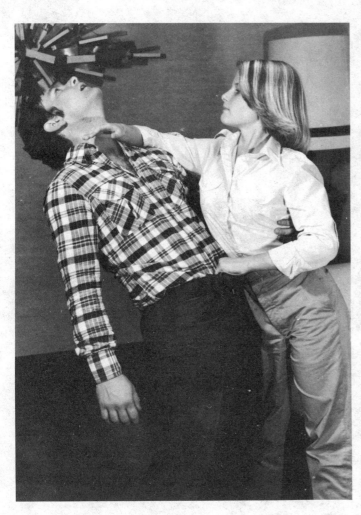

When an attacker drags his victim toward him, she should side-kick his knee with all her strength, drive her heel down his shinbone, and stomp his instep. If he falls to the ground, the victim can grasp his hair with both hands and smash her knee into his chin or face—breaking his jaw or knocking him out. If the attacker is still conscious, she can stomp him in the groin; this should finish him off.

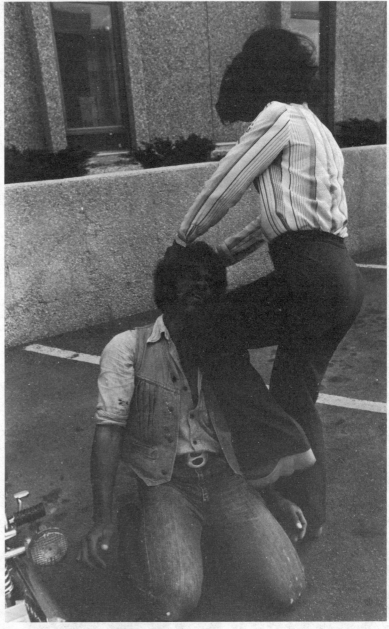

An alternative move, once the rapist has fallen, is for the victim to grasp the hair at the back of his head or the back of his collar and smash the knuckled-V fist into the bridge of his nose. Such a blow can be fatal if the bone is driven into the brain—which often happens in automobile accidents—and caution should be exerted when practicing with a partner.

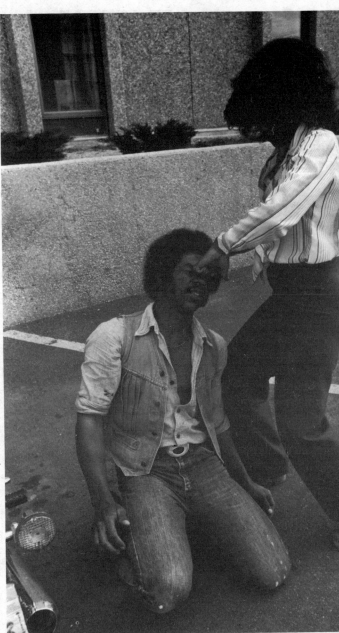

EPILOGUE

If I have succeeded in convincing only a small percentage of my readers that they *can* defend themselves against even the most aggressive rapist, then this book has been worth the effort. I have tried to emphasize several important points throughout my text in the hope that they might become more firmly fixed in the reader's mind. I would like to review those basic points here so that they will be handy for future reference, and so that you will leave RAPE — FIGHT BACK AND WIN! with them fresh in your memory.

1. The best way to ward off an attacker is to be prepared. Stay calm and think about what you have learned and practiced in this book. Then go into action!
2. Do not carry a gun, knife, or other deadly weapon with you for defensive purposes. It can be too easily turned against you by a stronger, more experienced enemy.
3. When attacked, use your voice, your hands, your knees, your house (or car) keys to frighten, hurt, and drive off your attacker.
4. If you are attacked by an armed rapist, do not try to defend yourself until or unless an opportunity arises to disarm the man and escape in safety.
5. Use your common sense at all times. Don't walk along lonely streets by yourself at night; vary your daily habits; keep your shades drawn at night.
6. When attacked in your home, throw something solid through the window, then yell FIRE as loud as you can. Do *not* scream RAPE!
7. Use the rapist's gullibility to lull him into believing that you will not resist — then bring my time-tested techniques into play!
8. A small, portable fire extinguisher is one of the best anti-rape weapons available. Carry one in your car at all times.
9. Remember, rape can happen anywhere and to anyone. Every woman is a potential victim. Be alert.
10. And finally, to all you parents and guardians, teach your children the *facts* about sex, so they can learn to distinguish between good and evil. Don't leave that all-important responsibility to your schools or your children's peers.

Thank you, and good luck.

Captain James A. Smith

MEET
THE
AUTHOR

Captain James A. Smith has been associated with law enforcement and defense techniques for over 25 years. He serves as the assistant chief of police and director of training for the Lake Charles (La.) Police Department, and is a member of the Louisiana Chiefs of Police Association. He is an active member of the International Association of Chiefs of Police and has served on the original Rape Crisis Bureau in Colorado Springs and El Paso County, Colorado. He is the author of many articles on rape defense and has appeared on national television and radio talk shows concerning the subject of rape. He has held seminars throughout the country and has lectured and taught more than 70,000 women about rape awareness and defensive tactics.

Captain Smith is also the National Director of the International Non-Lethal Weapons Association, a Certified State Instructor, and a member of the Justice Systems Training Association (JSTA), which provides information and training in defensive tactics for law enforcement officers throughout the U.S. Smith is a lifetime member of the Judo Black Belt Federation of the United States and is registered at the KODOKAN in Tokyo, Japan. He has taught more than 300 police departments how to use his new nonlethal humane weapon, known as the SOURCE, and is the recipient of the "Human Resources of America" award. He also serves as consultant to the El Paso County Sheriffs Department (Colo.), the Bellfontaine Police Department, and the Logan County Sheriffs Department in Ohio.